Software Engineering Process Models

(A Questionnaire Approach)

Software Engineering Process Models

(A Questionnaire Approach)

Deepak Jain

M.Tech.(CSE), B.Tech.(ECE)

Specialization: Object Oriented Software Engineering

Life Associate Member: Computer Society of India

BPB PUBLICATIONS

B-14 Connaught Place, New Delhi-110 001

FIRST EDITION 2007 REPRINTED 2011

ISBN 81-8333-191-2

Distributors:

MICRO BOOK CENTRE
2, City Centre, CG Road,
Near Swastic Char Rasta,
AHMEDABAD-380009 Phone: 26421611

COMPUTER BOOK CENTRE
12, Shrungar Shopping Centre, M.G. Road,
BANGALORE-560001 Phone: 25587923, 25584641

MICRO BOOKS
Shanti Niketan Building, 8, Camac Street,
KOLKATTA-700017 Phone: 22826518, 22826519

BUSINESS PROMOTION BUREAU
8/1, Ritchie Street, Mount Road,
CHENNAI-600002 Phone: 28410796, 28550491

DECCAN AGENCIES
4-3-329, Bank Street,
HYDERABAD-500195 Phone: 24756400, 24756967

MICRO MEDIA
Shop No. 5, Mahendra Chambers, 150 D.N. Road,
Next to Capital Cinema V.T. (C.S.T.) Station,
MUMBAI-400001 Ph.: 22078296, 22078297

BPB PUBLICATIONS
B-14, Connaught Place, **NEW DELHI-110001**
Phone: 23325760, 23723393, 23737742

INFO TECH
G-2, Sidhartha Building, 96 Nehru Place,
NEW DELHI-110019
Phone: 26438245, 26415092, 26234208

INFO TECH
Shop No. 2, F-38, South Extension Part-1
NEW DELHI-110049
Phone: 24691288

BPB BOOK CENTRE
376, Old Lajpat Rai Market,
DELHI-110006
PHONE: 23861747

Published by Manish Jain for BPB Publications, B-14, Connaught Place, New Delhi-110 001 a
Printed by him at Akash Press, New Delhi.

About Author

Author, Mr. Deepak Jain, based in Delhi, holds Master of Technology in Computer Science & Engineering from Centre for Development of Advanced Computing (Ministry of IT, Govt. of India), specialized in 'OOAD & Digital VLSI Designing'. Prior, he completed Bachelor of Technology in Electronics & Communication Engineering with specialization in 'Communication System & Antenna Applications' from Institute of Engineering & Technology, Kanpur, India.

He has working experience of teaching, R&D, Software Designing and FPGA developments. He has also rendered services to BPO and Banking sectors in India. He has published a number of research papers and articles in software designing, automation and VLSI Designing.

Mr. Jain is Life Associated Member of Computer Society of India. He is a Platinum member of Code-Project Group, a team to provide guidance to international researchers and developers with open source coding and project development. He is an active academician and researcher.

Dedication

To two,
who enrich my life
especially with their
love and blessings:

My wife

&

My mother

Acknowledgement

My thanks to many individuals who made possible to bring this first edition into its current structure, all people who contributed directly or indirectly, in preparation of this bound material and all those made me capable of doing this work. It may not be possible to specifically mention names of each of them because the world is full of supportive and obliging people and hundreds of them come forward when to take some step forward. One may not list them in a single go yet some of them can be name with the first thought.

Before all I acknowledge my wife Mrs. Deepa Jain, for her best support and regular guidance for preparation of the manuscript of this first edition. Without her regular motivation and reviewing guidance I could never come with this work. My heartiest respect goes to Mr. Manish Jain and his team of BPB Publications, who made release of this edition in record times. My special regards are for Ms. Chitra Kasana who was among the first few who appreciated my idea to come with description of software engineering principles in a questionnaire format that may be of great help for university students who, parallel to intend to know the principles and their practical applications, intend to score good in their examinations. Having an idea of types and structure of the probable questions in the subject could best help them to rise their scores high.

I thank to my brother, parents and family members for there extreme patience, support and encouragement. This bound document is result of hard work of several nights that we spent without sleep. Several heart touching events and happenings are attached with this. Same hand, this document holds iota of emotions and sentiments. I remember all those good and bad experiences and wish you happy reading.

Deepak Jain

Preface

'Software Engineering' was added as a core subject in most of undergraduate and postgraduate degree courses in information technology with a focus of providing practical and theoretical knowledge about the techniques and methodologies associated with its processes. Companies were always interested to work with experienced and mature manpower that have an exposure about the common practices of software development and their inbuilt complexities. With a goal of producing fresher work force with a fair idea of common software practices, many universities gave place to practices of software development in their core courses of professional studies.

But slowly, most of them lost their focus of providing both practical and theoretical experience of software processes. One of the most common reasons for this was unavailability of automated and semi-automated tools in software practices. Also, the academicians could not justify for proper case studies for their students that could allow them to explore and apply their theoretical knowledge for solving the practical problems. This left the 'Software Engineering' course moreover on a theoretical base and in most of the universities students were taught about theoretical aspects of its process and techniques.

Slowly, students also started taking this subject as a theoretical one and they lost their interest in its practical applicability. Finally, the common focus of universities and software companies of developing fresh work power with a pre-exposure to software practices lost its existence because the pure theories could never expose the complexities behind them.

Students should never forget that whatever they are learning in the class rooms, they are finally going to apply in their profession and the same it true for students of 'Software Engineering' also. Hence they should always look into the practical aspects of the theories they learn. Same head, the instructors, teachers and academicians need to give appropriate importance to practical works and case studies in software engineering and its practices. They should create environment to promote and enhance the vision of students in this course. They need to make the students understand the need to learn this course and its practical expectations in the recruiters.

I, as a regular academician, understand the parallel focus of students to score high in their exams and some or the other way, in most of the case, they take their theory exams as their weapon for this because in practical exams, the difference of the marks is not much between the competitor students. But in this fight of rank in class, generally students loose their focus of getting into the depth of the basic knowledge of the subject. To meet to both of the focus of students, i.e. the focus of scoring high in their theory exams by stating precise and accurate answers, and the focus of going into the depth of concept of software practices and process methodologies, I could rank the Questionnaire the best approach. The questionnaire can give the students a direct approach to the types of the questions important for their theory exams and can tell them the accurate and sufficient answers for high scores. On the same side, the well structured answers of these selected questions give them a feeling of the inherent complexities of the software practices as well as the solutions to these complexities.

The students of 'Software Engineering', while learning the subject, should put themselves in the process and feel the practical problems in the process. They need to assume themselves as parts of the process and need to understand the responsibilities of the executers of each step of the process. Once they will start placing them in the process and start feeling the practical processes, they can understand the visibility of the process and its products.

The students should work on as much case studies as they can. The case studies may be taken in a form of a problem in hand and software engineering principles may be applied on it in order to get a solution. In this manner, the students get the best exposure to the common complexities of the engineering practices in software development. They should also work with alternative solutions in order to compare their suitability for testing, enhancing, and maintaining the product. Moreover, better result can also be expected in a team work. Students should work in teams and each individual in the team should take up the responsibilities in a professional manner so that they can explore to meet the tight schedules, milestones and quality scales of the product.

About the current edition of the book

The book, 'Software Engineering Process Models: A Questionnaire Approach' has been produced with a focus of providing the readers a fair exposure of common software processes and their inherent activities. The in-hand bound stuff describes common complexities in the software development. The contents of the book are divided into two sections.

Section-I, 'Introduction to Software and Software Engineering' talks about the basic terminologies and definitions of software engineering and software engineering processes. This section is covered in tow chapters.

This section introduces the terms Software, Software Engineering, Software Development Life Cycle (SDLC), CAD and CASE. The section explains the roles of a software-engineer and major challenges in his job work. The current section makes the readers familiar with goals of software engineering and its work products. The cost of software engineering and complexities in software development are introduced in this section.

The section also compares the terms software engineering, computer science and computer engineering. It states major difference in software and hardware and their development processes and constraints. This section explains differences between software and a program as these are the terms generally used synonymously in spite of being two quite different terms. This section reveals the need of documentation in software and other constrains in software development.

The objective of section-I is to make the readers understand the basic terms and components in software engineering. The section aims in explaining the term software, software engineering, software engineering processes, role and challenges for software engineering and cost of software engineering. The major objective of this section includes making the readers understand the complexity of software development, its huge expenses and need of serious efforts for development of reliable and maintainable software timely under controlled costs.

Section-II, "Software Process Models" describes the facts about common software development processes in industry. This section is also covered in two chapters. This section included the definitions of software process and process model. This section introduces the terms Software Process, Software Process Models, Software Development Life Cycle (SDLC). The section explains different phases of software development process. In this section, the author collects the description of the steps involved in software development and the work product of each step. The common complexities and costs involved in each step are also summarized here in this part of the book.

The section describes the software process as an iterative and incremental process for development and implementation of the automation solutions for meeting the requirements of consumer. The section descries different phases of each of the iterations in the development process. Different focuses and goals of these phases are detailed herein. This section also summarizes a set of common risks involved in iterations.

The objective of this section is to make the readers understand the basic terminologies in a software process. The section aims in explaining the terms software process, software process iterations, inception, elaboration, construction, transition, and risk. The section focuses on explaining the focus and work output of each phase in software process and cost of each phase of software development process. Another objective of this section is to explain the common risk definitions and types of risks.

The book makes efforts to meet the requirements of students of different universities for scoring well by direct hitting the questions in right and precise manner. Objective is to introduce software engineering to readers to enable them to tackle the complexities of basic concepts of software engineering in a manner to answer a set of common questions about it.

Table of Content

Section-I

Introduction to Software and Software Engineering

Section-II

Software Development Process

Section-I

Introduction to Software & Software Engineering

Introduction to Section-I

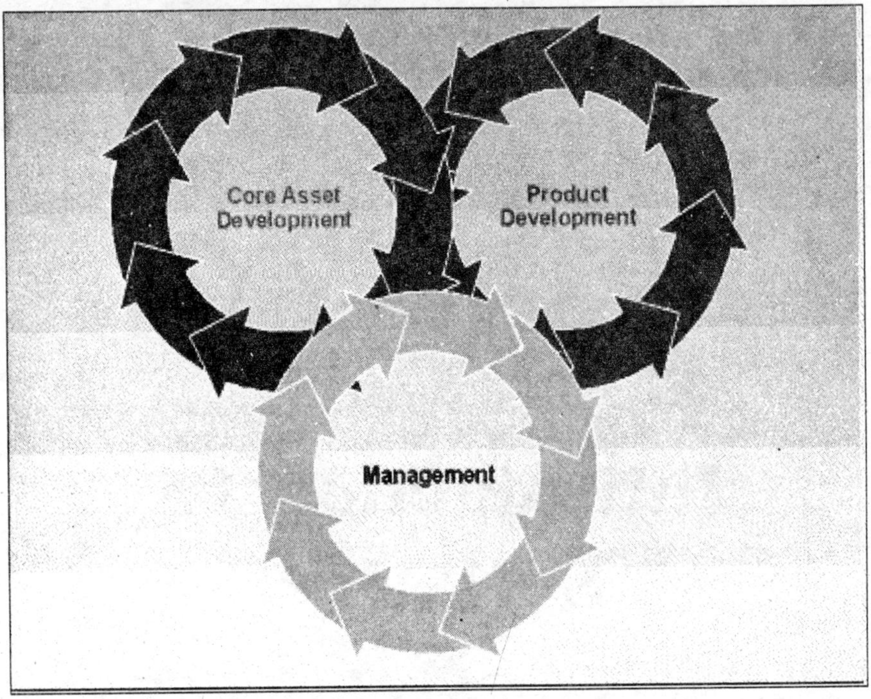

The Section-I introduces the terms Software, Software Engineering, Software Development Life Cycle (SDLC), CAD and CASE. The section explains the roles of a software-engineer and major challenges in his job work. The current section makes the readers familiar with goals of software engineering and its work products. The cost of software engineering and complexities in software development are introduced in this section.

The section also compares the terms software engineering, computer science and computer engineering. It states major difference in software and hardware and their development processes and constraints. This section explains differences between software and a program as these are the terms generally used synonymously in spite of being two quite different terms. This section reveals the need of documentation in software and other constrains in software development.

Objective

The objective of this section is to make the readers understand the basic terms and components in software engineering. The section aims in explaining the term software, software engineering, software engineering processes, role and challenges for software engineering and cost of software engineering. The major objective of this section includes making the readers understand the complexity of software development, its huge expenses and need of serious efforts for development of reliable and maintainable software timely under controlled costs.

1

Introduction

Software is no more as simple as they were in their earliest times. Most of our daily works are now depending on software working for us. Our mobile phones, information systems, memory systems, DTP systems, video games, CD players and even channel scan systems in our FM radio are working on some simple or complex software that support and supported by some hardware system associated with them. It may also be said that the software are running on hardware or controlling the hardware. With the increased complexities and cost of development of software, the traditional hit and trial methodologies of programming have lost their utility. The consumer expectations today are so complex that they need to be analyzed in depth in formal manner in order to understand them clearly or otherwise they lead to a failure of development. In order to meet the needs of today's huge software requirements, merely programming doesn't suffice the professional needs. Rather formal engineering principles are required to be applied for development of software. This leads to birth of software engineering as another branch of engineering profession that is dedicated to development, operation and maintenance of software product and betterment of development processes.

Q. 1. Define Software Engineering

IEEE defines 'Software Engineering' as

(1) application of systematic, disciplined, quantifiable approach to the development, operation and maintenance of software i.e. application of engineering to software and

(2) the study of approaches as in.

Software Engineering

Includes

Software Product	**Software Process**
Analysis of Software	Development of Process
Development of Software	Research of Software Process and Methodologies
Training of Software	Enhancement of Development Processes
Operation of Software	Management Control over Technology
Maintenance of Software	

Figure 1.1: Software Engineering Focus Activities

Software engineering may also be defined as the disciplined application of engineering, scientific, and mathematical principles, methods, and tools to the economical production of quality software. Software Engineering is the technology discipline concerned with developing large computer software applications. Software engineering covers not only the technical aspects of building software systems, but also management issues, such as directing programming teams, scheduling, and budgeting. According to Fritz Bauer, it is the establishment and use of sound engineering principles in order to obtain reliable and efficient software economically. Software Engineering (SE) is a profession dedicated to creation and maintenance of software applications by applying technologies and practices from computer science, project management, engineering, application domains and other fields.

Software engineering, like traditional engineering disciplines, deals with issues of cost and reliability. Some software applications contain millions of lines of code that are expected to perform properly in the face of changing conditions, making them comparable in complexity to the most complex modern machines.

Q. 2. What is the role/responsibility of a software engineer?

Software Engineer is responsible for designing and programming large-scale computer systems and applications. Similar to a systems analyst, software engineer primarily designs and builds complex system software such as operating systems, protocol architectures, or databases upon which application software programs will run.

Software engineer needs to model the requirements and expectation of the software into formal symbols and representations of specifications. It needs to create architecture of the system and blue-prints for the design of the software modules and their interconnections. One is expected to write building programs implementing the design and test plans to have checks on possible errors. Software engineer is an active member of the software developing team and needs to cope well with the team members and leaders & controllers. Software engineers are responsible for the success of the software and in practice; most of the organizations divide the responsibilities among several specialists as per their area of specialization and command.

Software engineer must of course be good in programming, algorithm analysis and data structure concepts. The person is expected to be familiar with different design approaches and capable to translate consumer-requirements and expectations to precise formal technical specifications. Software person is expected to be equipped with good communication and interpersonal soft skills. It also needs the abilities of schedule and control work for itself as well as that for others in the team because Software Engineering is a sum out of team work only dedicated to a common goal.

Q. 3. What are the major challenges before the software engineers?

Major challenges before software engineers:

1. **Overshooting cost of software development:** The major challenge for the software engineers is the up shooting costs of software. In spite of extreme planning, research, analysis, management and control, software overshoots their costs of development and maintenance. Software is more expensive to develop as compared to hardware when produced in mass.

2. **Knowledge of design approach:** A number of design approaches are available in practices to convert a set of specifications into precise architecture and implementation. It may be quite mystifying for a human to choose for the approach for the best results. Software-engineers are required to possess knowledge and experience of all the design approaches which are able to converse with the user of the system in terms of applications.

3. **Knowledge of development process models:** Software engineer are required to have knowledge and experience of different process models that can be used for development of the system in an efficient manner. They are expected to choose among the number of available process model for an appropriate model according to the conditions, limitations and environment

of the problem in hand. Software engineers face challenges of modifying or building models to use them to answer the queries about the behavior of the system, its performance and other characteristics at different phases of development.

4. **Handling the project at abstraction levels:** Software engineers face a big challenge of moving among several stages of abstraction at different stages of development. Software engineers manage the projects from highest level of abstraction at specification, to abstraction of software design and detailed design.

5. **Measuring and planning the project:** Software engineer have continuously facing problems in measuring the attributes viz. size, duration, documentation, cost, difficulty of development, man power required and complexity of a project. The project is generally planned on the estimations of its attributes in early phases of development. But for many unavoidable reasons, generally, these projects overshoot

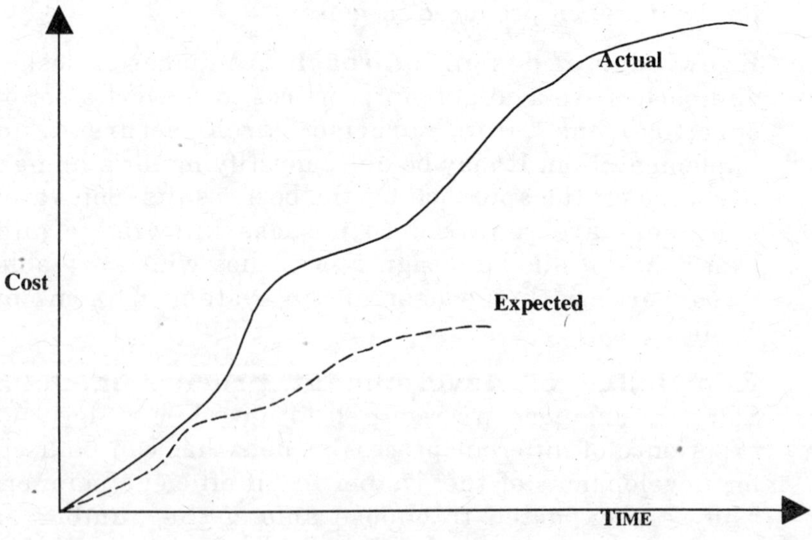

Figure 1.2: Cost & Time Overshooting for S/W Development

in the durations, costs and efforts. Software engineers have been facing challenges in measuring or estimating the attributes of the project close to their practical values.

Q. 4. How is Software Engineering different from Computer Engineering and Computer Science?

Computer Engineering concerns mainly with the practical details of efficiently applications of existing computer technology. Here technology refers to both hardware and software. Thus, computer engineering deals with the fundamentals of computer design. It is a study of the design, construction, and testing of both basic and sophisticated computing machines. It may also include learning of computer communications and networking, including the Internet. In other words, computer engineering is the branch of engineering that deals with hardware and software technology, their development and relationships.

Computer engineering also include some parts of software development but not to the extent as that is included in computer science. This is where the overlap with computer science comes in. Computer Engineers are expected to have expertise in all aspects of computers including the hardware transistor circuit right up to the successful design of software user interfaces. This means that the computer engineer is supposed to have knowledge of a computer system at all abstract levels right from highest abstraction of user-interface to its implementation in bit format leading to its hardware implementation in terms of voltages and currents.

Computer Science is the field of applied science concerned with the efficient application of technology of computing by designing the efficient algorithms and the ways to organize and store the information. Usually a computer scientist needs not to have knowledge of Electrical Engineering or the hardware components of the computer system. They mostly deal for the software theory and application area of computer technology. This means that computer science mostly deals with computational theories and algorithm analysis and designs related to computer executions.

For a long time, there has been a belief of taking computer science related to software engineering as the way physics and chemistry are related to traditional engineering. Some others have belief that software engineering is an engineering discipline. The fact is that software has become a larger and more important part of any computer systems. It has also become complicated and requires large teams of resources and time to get developed. Consequently, the discipline of software engineering has emerged. Software engineering focuses on the design, analysis, and management of large-scale software systems. Software engineering is a formal application of engineering, scientific and mathematical principles to order to develop, test, use and maintain economic and efficient software.

Here is another way to look at it:

- Computer engineering is about building computers.
- Computer science is about programming computers.
- Software engineering is about assembling large programs.

Q. 5. What are the goals of software engineering?

As per the definition of Software Engineering, its goal is to produce quality software in economical manner that can work efficiently and reliably in the real environment. The software engineering is dedicated to producing the cost effective and timely solutions for automation and control of critical processes with the help of software enhanced in the quality, reliability and security. Moreover, software engineering is not confined merely to development of software products. It is also concerned to the improvement in the process of development, control over the process and management of the product. Software engineering is also aimed to enhancement in the quality of its work product and lowering its cost by better management and usage of modern tools. Software engineering is focused towards better consumer satisfaction and services. Software engineering has goals of producing user friendly software with high reliability, efficiency, clarity, testability, maintainability, and robustness. Its scope spans to enhancement of the control over the development process to reduce effort consumption, resource consumption and time consumption in software development. It aims to reduce the complexity of development process, better understanding of user requirements, reducing ambiguities and misconceptions of designs, reducing complexity of implementation, enhancing the scope and effectiveness of testing, provide user satisfactory developments and maintaining the development products.

Q. 6. Explain the work products of software engineering?

Software engineering work products may be listed as follows:

- **Reusable work product**: They include the artifacts produced during development procedure. They include the modules; reusable files, interfaces and other logical products developed for required functioning of the system.
- **Internal work product**: These are the work product produced for a project's internal consumption. They include the data storage designs, internal memory architecture, temporary stored information etc.
- **Deliverable work product**: These are the work product for a client, specified prior to the start of the project and written into a contract. They include the documentation, data structure and the integrated software program along with all its functioning components.

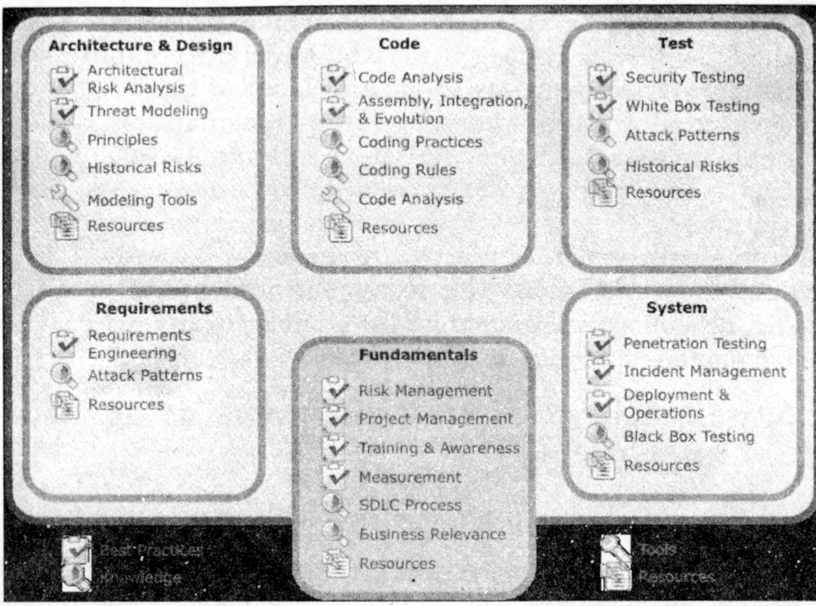

Figure 1.3: General areas of application of Software Engineering

Q. 7. What are the costs of software engineering?

Costs of software engineering across the development process depend on the technique or the process adopted for the development. Cost distribution over the complete process may be stated where the cost of specifications, designing, development, testing and maintenance are measure separately. But generally, as the software development is an iterative process with no precise line of separation between its phases in early stages, it becomes tough to measure the cost of each step separately. But, with long researches and watches over a number of projects, it is found that generally integration and testing of the system are the most expensive activities of the development process and consume 40 to 50 percent of the total development cost. Requirement elicitation, designing and implementation phases respectively consume 12%, 20% and 18% of the total cost of development. While budgeting for the project, some resources are allotted to post development services (maintenance activities) also.

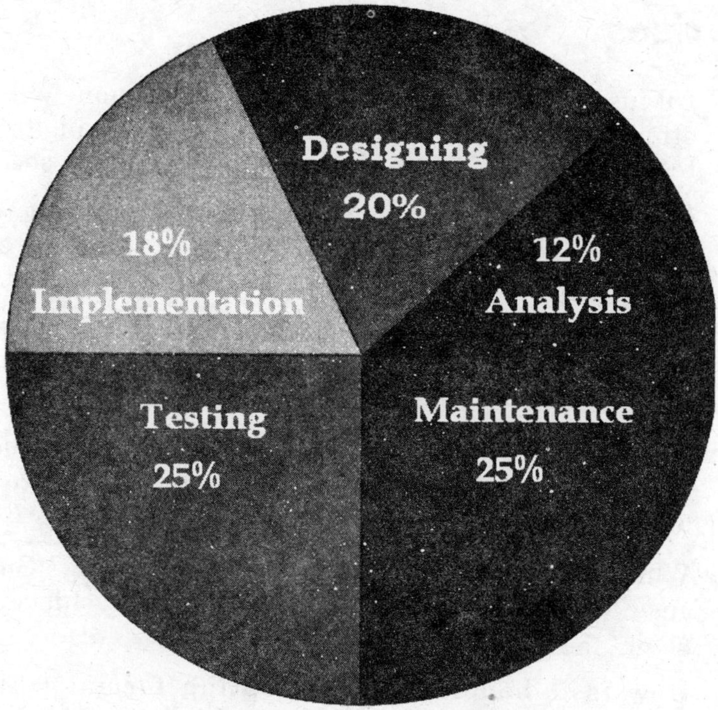

Figure 1.4: Cost of Software Engineering

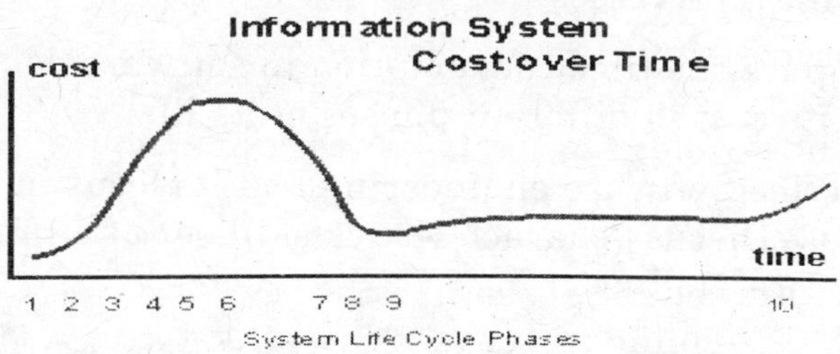

1. System Inception
2. Project Initiation
3. Requirements
4. System
5. Software Design
6. Construction
7. Testing
8. Deployment
9. Production
10. Termination

Figure 1.5: Cost of Information System vs. Time

Exercises

i. Discuss software engineering as a profession. What are ethical responsibilities of a software engineering towards technical and non technical components of the society?

ii. Can you think of probable disastrous impacts of software engineering? Suggest what should be done to avoid/ control ruinous effects of software engineering?

iii. What are the major challenges before the software engineers? Can you suggest some controlling steps to be taken or some solutions to these challenges?

iv. How are the terms Software Engineering, Computer Engineering and Computer Science related to each others? How are they serving to each others?

v. What are the goals of software engineering? Suggest some common practices or approaches to achieve these goals?

vi. How is it beneficial for adopting formal software engineering practices in software development? How can software engineering give a management control over technical processes?

vii. Compare the time consumption in software development and its cost in different phases of its life.

viii. Describe Software engineering and its focus in your own words. Discuss characteristics skill set of a professional software engineer.

ix. Discuss some common conflicts between software engineers and management controlling the software development in an organization.

x. State and explain some common myths in software engineering industry.

xi. What are the costs of software engineering? Why is software development considered to be costlier than hardware manufacturing?

2

The Software

There was a time when most of the human needs were based on hardware like wheel, wooden and iron weapons etc. Later, automation of processes lied on electrical appliances like fan, transformers and coils. But hardwired automation was proved to be too rigid to be changed or modified whenever require. This led to adoption of computer programs based automations and solutions. Slowly, the expectations and requirements of the consumer went more and more complex. This led to need to make the programs not only correct and reliable but also maintainable and lasting long. Also the requirements of special training for users and formal development and delivery of the software were faced with increased complexities of software. Modern software developments are no more mere programs to perform some task but much more than that.

Q. 1. Define Software. Explain different constitutes of software.

Software is something that the software engineers design and develop. It encompasses programs that execute within a computer of any size and architecture, documents that encompass hardcopy and virtual forms, and data that encompasses numbers and text, but also includes representations of pictorial, video, and audio information. *Software* is an integrated collection of Programs, Data Structure and any associated documentation pertaining to the operation of a system.

- ***Program*** is a set of instructions or written coded commands that tells a computer what tasks to perform and controls the operation of a computer.
- ***Data Structure*** is the description of the way in which information is organized in a system i.e. the way the data is organized to ensure efficient processing. This may be in lists, arrays, stacks, queues or trees. At the broadest level, data structure includes definitions of entire entities or files or related items.
- ***Documentation*** cover any document (hardcopy or softcopy) which defines the functional requirements, standards, methods, design, procedures, implementation, test, operation or support arrangements that pertain to a software item or any data used by a software item.

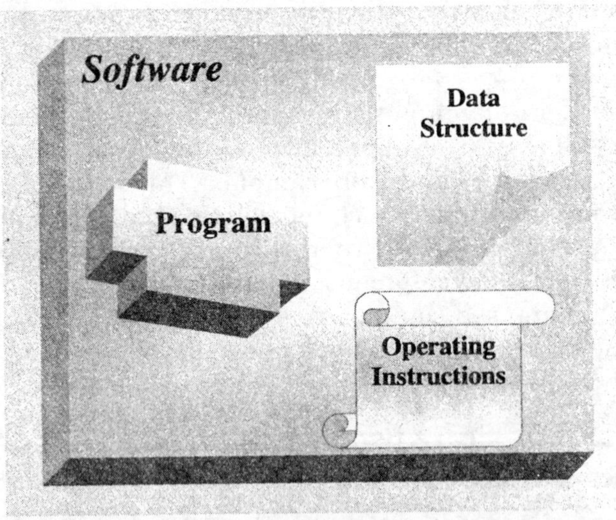

Figure 2.1: Software Constituents

Q. 2. State the key differences between characteristics of Software and Hardware.

Computer systems are the integration of hardware and software components. Here the hardware represents the tangible hard components of the system whereas the term software means to the intangible data, information, signals, program components and interfaces. The two components of the computer system work in collaboration to achieve the commonly defined tasks but the characteristics of the two components differ by big differences.

1. Software include logical or intangible components of the system like the computer-programs, data stores, information, data structure, documentation, operating system, driver programs, on-screen user interfaces etc. On the other hand, the hardware include the physical or tangible components like motherboard, monitor screen, keyboards, cables, mouse, joy stick, switching system etc.

2. Software is engineered whereas Hardware is manufactured. Although, the two terms may seem to be similar but the approach of development is different. The major difference lay in the approach of designing and implementation of the design. Software is an outcome of analysis, design and coding with an understanding of constraints of its user-type, use-type, programming environment, lifetime etc. On the other hand, the hardware developments are based of data unit and control unit designs. These systems are defined in terms of data lines (or data bus) and control lines (or control bus). Hardware development constraints are clock-speed, setup time, hold time, inertial & transport delays, temperature, humidity and other physical conditions etc.

3. Software does not face energy related wear out while use, just like hardware. Encountering with the physical contacts and motion against fictitious surfaces of contact, the hardware modules of any system face the losses of wearing and tearing. But software, being a set of logical

(non physical) components, don't face such losses. In fact, software does not wear while use but they deteriorate while maintenance and enhancements according to the changed technologies and demands. This means that the software have tendency to accumulate defects as the time pass due to errors being introduced during maintenance. Hardware where follow a bath tub shape of graph of failure as shown in the Figure 2.3, software, on the other hand, show spikes for deterioration, shown in Figure 2.4.

4. Cost of software usually does not fall down in bulk production as in case of hardware. This is because of the fact that the hardware components are manufactured with the same pattern, design and requirement. On the other hand, software products are custom build. The requirements of different users of the software may be similar but not the same. The modifications in the software for its customization to make it adapted with the changed expectations raise is cost even if it is in bulk production. This is the reason why we call software is developed whereas hardware is manufactured.

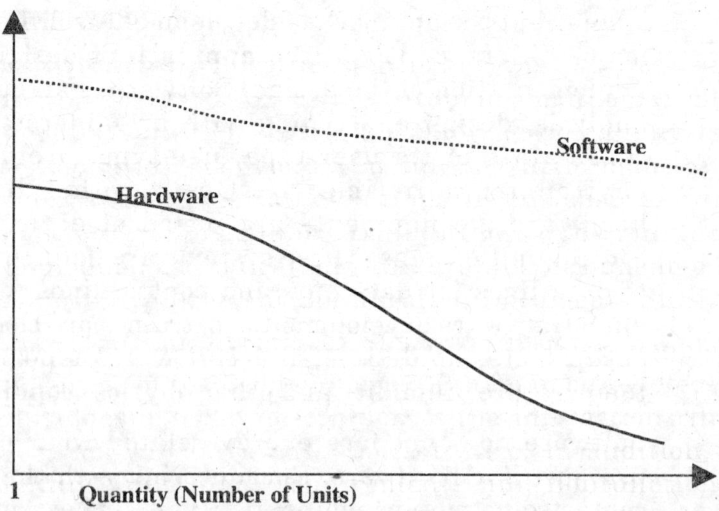

Figure 2.2: Effect on per unit cost in case of bulk manufacturing of H/W vs. S/W

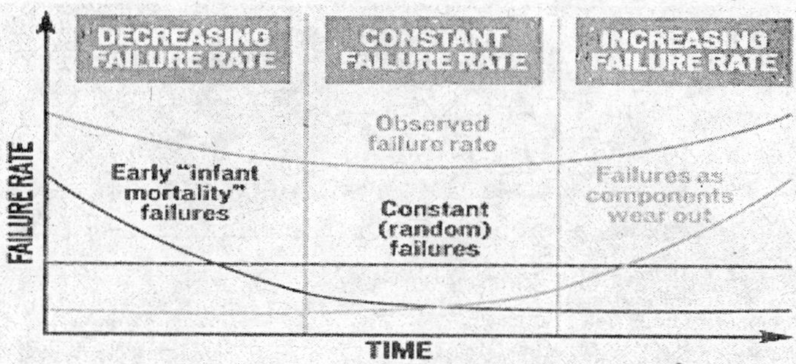

Figure 2.3: Failure rate for Hardware Components

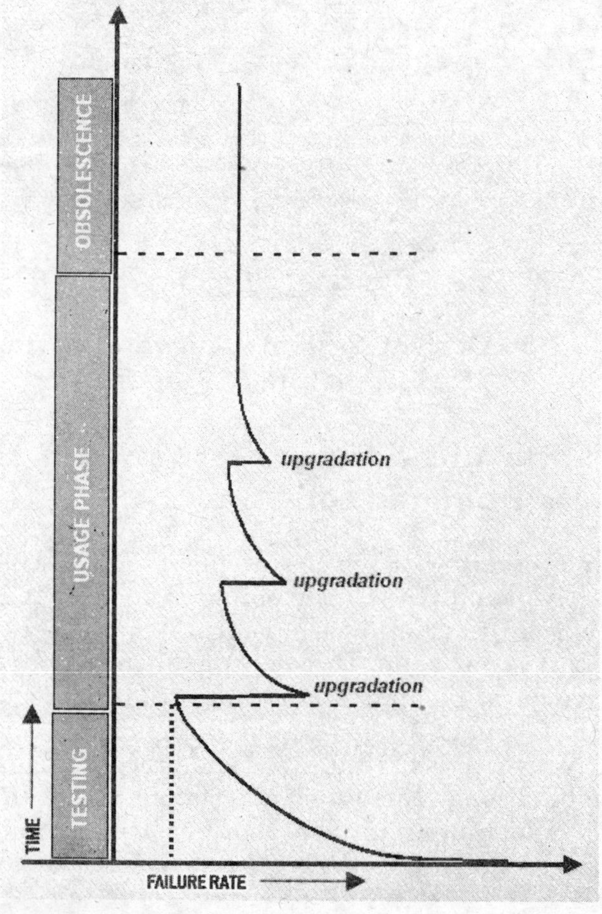

Figure 2.4: Failure rate for Software

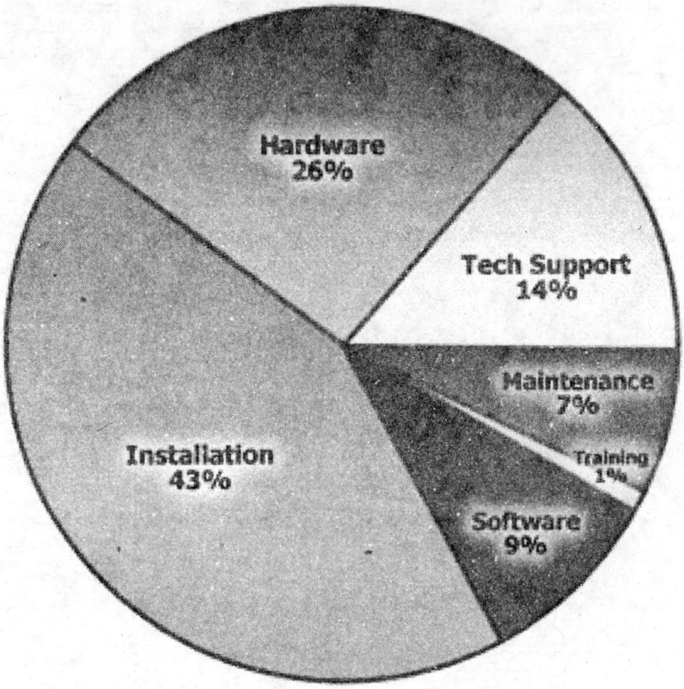

Figure 2.5: Cost of System (Software + Hardware) Development & Release

Q. 3. State the differences between computer program and software.

Computer program is a set of statements or instructions to be used directly or indirectly in a computer in order to bring about a certain result. Computer Program may be taken as an intermediary between the computer hardware and the informative data. Computer program is that part of a computer system that consists of encoded information (or computer instructions) which is used to store and process this information. It is a combination of computer instructions and data definitions that enable computer hardware to perform computational or control functions.

On the other hand, Software includes data structure and documentation along with the computer programs in it. Software is an integrated collection of Programs, Data Structure and any associated documentation pertaining to the operation of a system.

Here data means to any information that has either been input to the system or output from the system or generated within the system during the processing or executions. The data structure represents the structures in which the data about the system or for the system has been organized. The data here means to both the external and internal information required for the smooth working for the system.

The documentation is for describing the usage, mode of operations, requirement specifications, quick references to important terms, test plans, maintenance plans, suggestions etc. They play important role in installing the software, learning its usage and operation, organizing information about its working, enhancing or up grading its functionality and the quality of its results and also in the development of suitable replacement when and as required in future.

Q. 4. Discuss different complexities and troubles serving as bottleneck in software development.

Different complexities faced by the developers and costumer in the software development procedure may be summarized as follows:

- **Communication gap:** Software developers and end users often have different vocabularies. Consequently, they can believe they are in perfect agreement until the finished product is supplied. Due to their own beliefs and expectations about the system, both face problems in describing their views and constraints to each other. Further, the communication with users is slow and users often do not participate in reviews or are incapable of doing so being technically unstable.

- **Hard to meet changing expectations:** Usually, when the project is started, the Users don't understand what they want and also they won't commit to a set of written requirements. Users insist on new requirements after the cost and schedule have been fixed. This commonly leads to the situation where user requirements keep changing even when the software development has been started. Because new requirements may sometimes mean changing the technology as well, the importance of finalizing user requirements before the commencement of development should be made very clear to the Business Users. Knowing their objectives and expectations regarding the solution beforehand and documenting agreed requirements is fundamental to the success of a project.
- **Time overshooting:** Software development is not purely automated and fully controlled procedure. It is full of uncertainties and risks. The software is analyzed, designed and developed with intensive care yet lot of errors and faults are in built in that. These errors are discovered during testing and then removed. The process generally overshoots in time as was estimated in the contract. Also, accommodating the changed user-requirements and expectations puts the schedule off track.
- **Cost overshoots:** Usually, the project contract is mentioned with an estimated cost of development. The costumer expected the cost not to overshoot much beyond expectations but it does. This is because of all uncertainties inbuilt in the development procedure. Untimely changes in requirements of the customer, delayed encounter of error, lack of design maintainability, uncertainty of man power & resource availability and many more may be the reasons for this.
- **Hard to test:** The software is analyzed, designed and developed with intensive care yet lot of errors and faults are in built in that. Testing is a very expensive, time consuming, partly intuitive and largely systematic task.

Testing the system for each and every possible input is impractical. Efficiency and effectiveness of the set of test cases to cover every part of the system depends mainly on the analytical capability, experience and maturity of the tester and that of the testing tools involved in the process. Finding all the errors present in the system is almost impossible. Further, locating the detected errors and removing them is even more hard-hitting. Even the most rigorous testing cannot certify the system to be error free.

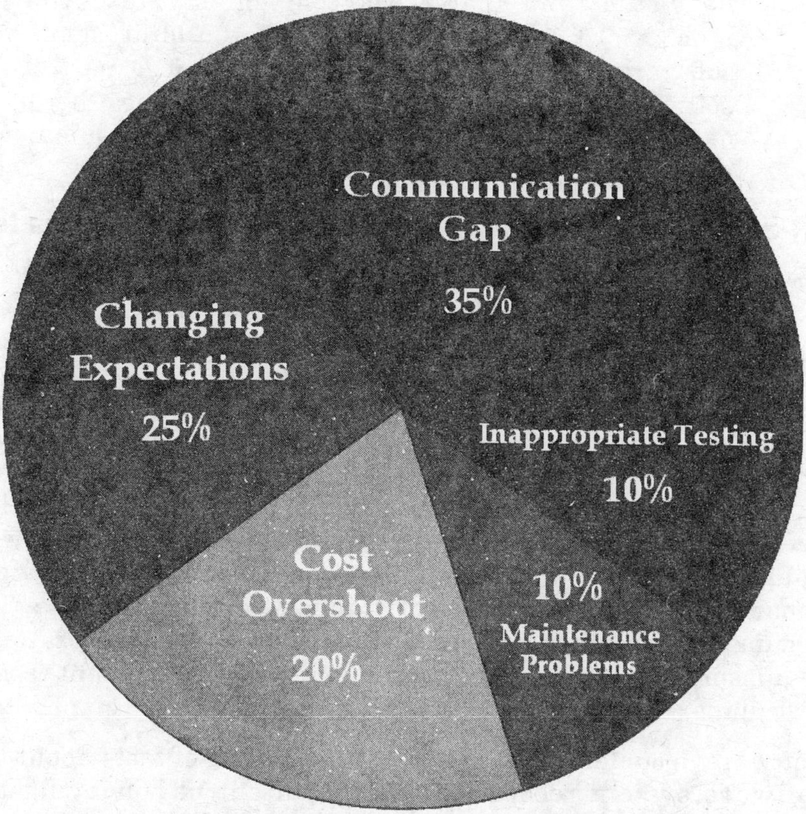

Figure 2.6: Software Failure rates due to complexities in Software Development

- **Hard to maintain:** After spending a fairly good amount of money on the development and usage of a software, it is not sensible to discard it and order for another new software merely to accommodate the enhanced requirements or up gradation in technology of the hardware or the communication media. Rather, up gradation in the software as per the new technology and expectations are desirable and hence maintenance of the software becomes very important for betters customer satisfaction. But to up grade the software, it is required to re-study and analyze the complete software which is much more cumbersome task than building some new software. Further, making any change in a part of the software usually reflects adverse effects in the other parts of the system. The software shows deterioration on each upgradation handling which is a hard task.

Q. 5. What is Software Documentation? Why is the documentation an important constituent of the software?

Software documentation is a document (hardcopy or softcopy) which defines the functional requirements, standards, methods, design, procedures, implementation, test, operation or support arrangements that pertain to a software item or any data used by a software item. Software Documentation is written text that accompanies computer software. It either explains how it operates or how to use it. In fact, the term software documentation means different things to different people. The documentation is for describing the usage, mode of operations, requirement specifications, quick references to important terms, test plans, maintenance plans, suggestions etc.

Software documentation is the written record of facts about the software system recorded with the intent of conveying the purpose, content and clarity. In documentation, an important (and often overlooked) task is documenting the internal design of software for the purpose of future maintenance and enhancement. Documentation is most important for external interfaces. Documentation is used to provide information in addition to that found on the application. An important need for auxiliary documentation is to document those aspects of the design that are difficult to extract directly from the design itself. These documents serve as a main guide to the developer to maintain the system in long terms. The documents contain technical and practical details about the prerequisites for use of the system and guidelines to use the system, which serve as fair trainers to the users. Documentation serves as baseline for usability of the system.

Documentation is an important part of software engineering that is often overlooked. They play important role in installing the software, learning its usage and operation, organizing information about its working, enhancing or up grading its functionality and the quality of its results and also in the development of suitable replacement when and as required in future.

Types of documentation include:

- Analyzer Output - SRS Document
- Architecture Outputs- Architectural overview of software; including relations to an environment, construction principles to be used in design and technical documentation, etc.
- Design Output- The design of software components.
- Technical Documentation Output - Documentation of code, algorithms, interfaces, APIs.
- End User Documentation Output - Manuals for the end-user.
- Operator Documentation Output - Manuals for the systems administrator.
- Application operator Documentation Output - Manuals for the "super-user" of the software.
- Help desk Documentation Output - Manuals for first and second line support.

Q. 6. Explain the terms CAD and CASE.

Computer-aided design (CAD) is the use of computers in industrial design applications such as architecture, engineering, and manufacturing. CAD tool is an automated system for the designing, drafting and display of graphically oriented information. Computer-aided software engineering (CASE) is the use of software tools to assist in the development and maintenance of software. Tools used to assist in this way are known as CASE Tools.

Many definitions and descriptions of CASE exist. CASE may be defined as the use of computer-based support in the software development process. This definition includes all kinds of computer-based support for any of the managerial, administrative, or technical aspects of any part of a software project. A CASE tool is a computer-based product aimed at supporting one or more software engineering activities within a software development process. A CASE environment is a collection of CASE tools and other components together with an integration approach that supports most or all of the interactions that occur among the environment components, and between the users of the environment and the environment itself.

Exercises

i. Define the term software and explain its constituting elements.

ii. What are the key differences between characteristics of Software & Hardware? What are the major differences in their production techniques of software and hardware?

iii. Do you think, the software development is much complex than mere programming? Explain.

iv. State some major differences between computer program and software. What are the key differences in the roles of programmer, software developer and software engineer?

v. Discuss some common complexities faced by programmers in industry. Explain why IT projects fail so often as compared to other projects.

vi. Discuss the complexities or troubles in software development. Explain the role of CASE tools to overcome these complexities.

vii. What is Software documentation? Discuss the importance of documentation after release of the software. What are major bottlenecks in development of quality documentations for software?

viii. What do you understand by software characteristic?

ix. What do you mean by good software? What are the expected quality-attributes of good software?

x. Explain the role of CAD & CASE tools in solving common myths in software industry.

xi. Discuss why documentation is an inseparable component of software. Explain the importance of software documents.

xii. Generally, program codes while programming are supported with many comment lines in it. Can these lines be considered taken as a part of software documentation?

Is software documentation different form commenting the programs?

xiii. What are common components of software documentations? What are their roles in software development life cycle? Can you categorize them on the basis of their importance for User, developer and both?

xiv. List out some common software you have used. Can you categorize them in system software, application software and designing/CASE tools? Are there any other classes to accommodate your choices?

xv. Explain the information and validity of the information depicted by the failure graphs of software and hardware as shown in figure:

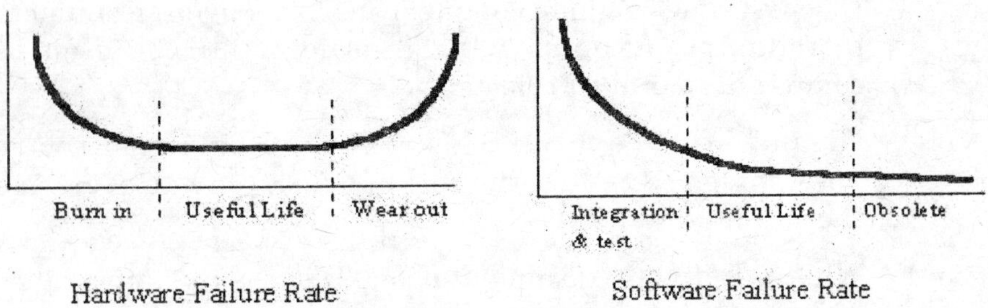

Figure 2.7: Failure rates in Software and Hardware Life Cycle

Section- II

Software Development Process

Introduction to Section-II

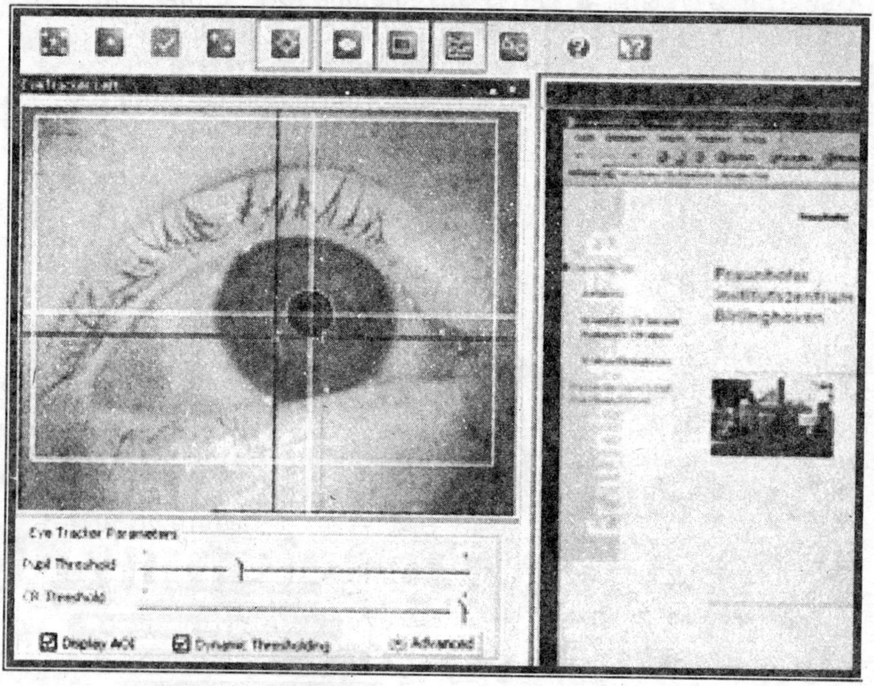

The Section-II introduces the terms Software Process, Software Process Models, Software Development Life Cycle (SDLC). The section explains different phases of software development process. In this section, the author collects the description of the steps involved in software development and the work product of each step. The common complexities and costs involved in each step are also summarized here in this part of the book.

The section describes the software process as an iterative and incremental process for development and implementation of the automation solutions for meeting the requirements of consumer. The section descries different phases of each of the iterations in the development process. Different focuses and goals of these phases are detailed herein. This section also summarizes a set of common risks involved in iterations.

Objective

The objective of this section is to make the readers understand the basic terminologies in a software process. The section aims in explaining the terms software process, software process iterations, inception, elaboration, construction, transition, and risk. The section focuses on explaining the focus and work output of each phase in software process and cost of each phase of software development process. Another objective of this section is to explain the common risk definitions and types of risks

3

Software Process

In many a ways, software development is same as any other development like building a house or making a bridge. The basic idea in all developments is to understand the needs, plan the things, implement the plan, test the development and hand over to the consumer. All the developments start with some need and the first step is to understand the need and then plan how to meet those needs. In planning, all the available resources and required resources are compared for having a feasibility check and the needed resources are managed. A blueprint for the implementation is planned and mapped with present and future needs. An appropriate plan is prepared on the basis of many comparisons for the best results. The plan is then executed by the application of methods and tools in order to implement the development. The results of development are then compared with the plan and errors are corrected. The final quality development is then handed over to the stakeholder for operation.

Similar to all other types of development, software developments are analyzed, planned, designed, implemented and tested before delivery. Each of the steps of the development process has a defined focus and objective and is executed in order to meet its objective in the best manner. Each step consume costs and resources and has its own importance in the process and hence needs care while execution.

Whenever the software fails, it is a failure of the process and not of the product. It is the failure of the efforts of development and the developing team. It is a failure of plan under execution. And after all, the final bearers are the developers and customer together. All processes hence need predictable, controllable and traceable characteristics that can be planned.

Q. 1. Define the term "Software Development Process".

A long history of software development has been focused to find repeatable, predictable processes that improve productivity and quality. Many organizations made efforts to formalize the seemingly informal software development. Some other institutions tried project management techniques to develop software. Without proper planning of the development procedure, software projects fear of the problems of over budget and over time. A large number of developments also face problems in meeting their expectations in terms of functionality, cost and delivery schedules. In order to meet all these problems in software development, the development procedure has been defined in the form of some formal steps that collectively are known as software development process.

Software development process (or simply software process) may be defined as a set of activities, methods and practices that are used in the production and evolution of software. Software process is a set of partially ordered steps intended to reach a goal in software engineering the goal is to build a software product or enhance an existing one. In short, software process is the total set of software engineering activities needed to transform the user's requirements into software.

A software development process is concerned primarily with the production aspect of software development, as opposed to the technical aspect. These processes exist primarily for supporting the management of software development, and are generally skewed toward addressing business concerns.

Software process defines the framework and a comprehensive plan for a set of Key Process Areas (KPAs) that must be established for effective delivery of software development technology. The KPA form the basis for management-control of software projects and establish the context in which technical methods are applied, work products are produced, milestones are established, quality is ensured and changes are properly managed.

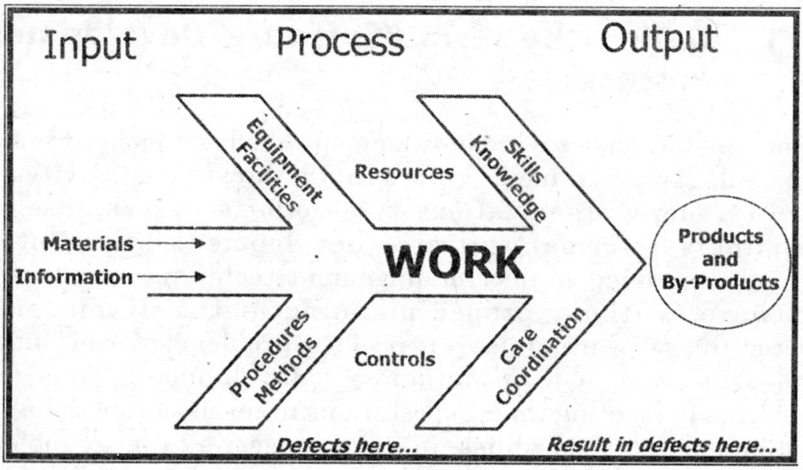

Figure 3.1: The Engineering Process

In short, software development process if the set of framework activities that can be applied to all software development projects regardless of their size and complexities. These framework activities include system engineering, setting project milestones, setting work-products, quality assurance activities, activities of maintenance and support etc

Q. 2. Discuss different activities involved in a general software development process.

A software-process is a set of activities, methods and practices that are used in the production and evolution of software. Software process is a set of partially ordered steps intended to reach a goal in software-engineering the goal is to build a software product or enhance an existing one. Software development requires performing many tasks that may be summarized as follows:

- **Feasibility Analysis:** The development process starts when some customer comes with a problem or requirement of automation of some process or service. The problem in hand is first of analyzed for its expected budget, time, reliability, durability, usability, compatibility with existing system/environment and its necessity in the scenario. According to all constraints, the practicality of development, installation and usage of the system are analyzed and evaluated in real time.

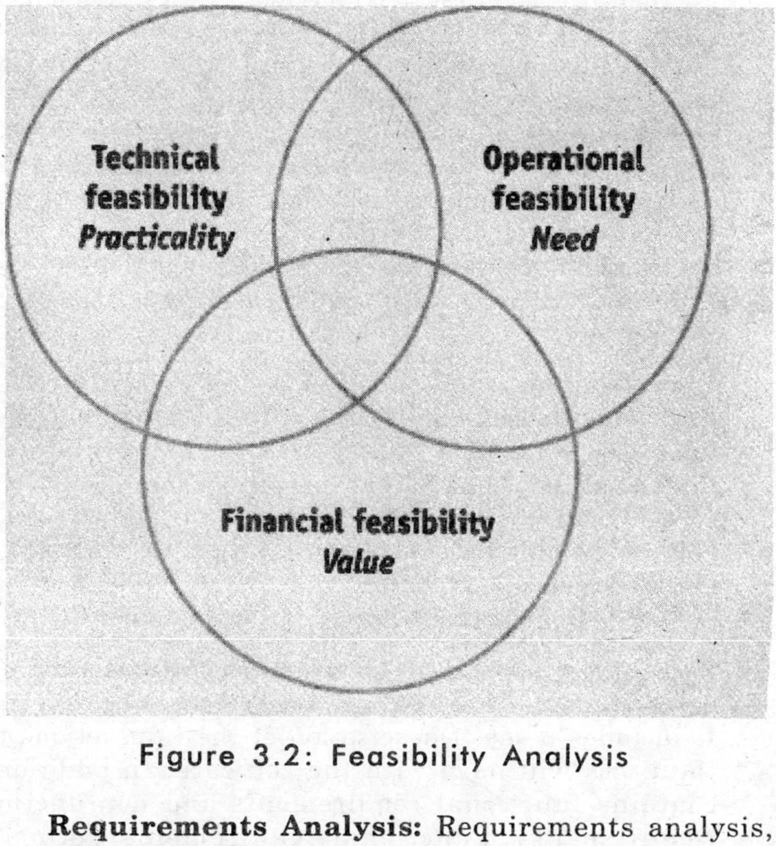

Figure 3.2: Feasibility Analysis

- **Requirements Analysis:** Requirements analysis, in software engineering, is a term used to describe all the tasks that go into the investigation, scoping and definition of a new or altered computer system. Requirements analysis is an important part of the software engineering process; whereby business analysts or software developers identify the requirements and expectations of a client. Requirements analysis is also known by different other names like *requirements engineering*, *requirements gathering*, *requirements capture*, *operational concept documenting*, *systems analysis*, *requirements specification* etc.

Requirement Analysis activities lead to extracting the requirements and expectations of a desired software product. It is the first task in Software Development Life Cycle. While customers probably believe they know what the software is to do, it may require skills and experience in software engineering to recognize incomplete, ambiguous or contradictory requirements. To understand the nature of the software, the engineer must understand the information domain of the software and its required set of functionalities, its behavior in real environment, performance expectations and interfaces & communications with other components of the environment.

- **Specification:** Specification is the task of precisely describing the software to be written in a mathematically rigorous way. The informal knowledge about the functionalities, behavioral expectations, performance and reliability needs as gathered from the customer and the consumer needs to be translated to formal and unambiguous specifications that are well documented in Software Requirement Specification Document (SRSD).

  A *software requirements specification* (SRS) is a complete description of the behavior of the system to be developed. It includes a set of description of the interactions that the users will have with the software. In addition, it contains functional requirements and nonfunctional requirements. Functional requirements define the internal workings of the software, i.e. the calculations, technical details, data manipulation & processing and other relevant functionality. Nonfunctional requirements impose constraints on the design or implementation such as performance requirements, quality standards, or design constraints.

In reality, most successful specifications are written to understand and fine-tune applications that were already well-developed. Specifications are most important for external interfaces that must remain stable.

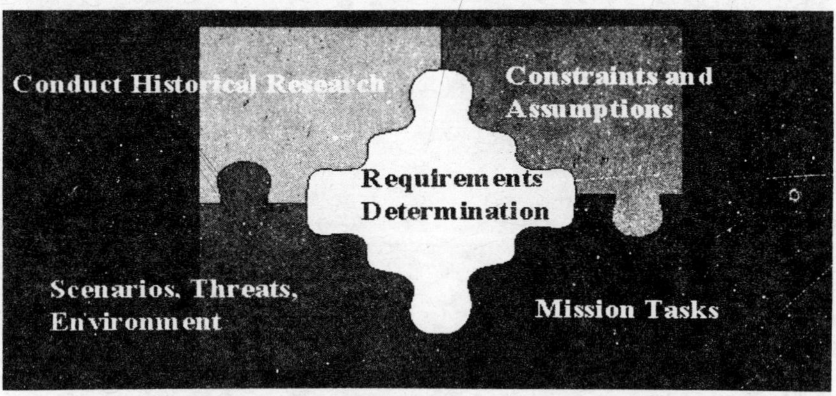

Figure 3.3: Requirement Analysis Activities

- **Design and Architecture:** Design activity transforms the functional specifications of the system into abstract structural specifications. Design and architecture refer to determining how software is expected to function in a general way without being involved in details. Design is the process of defining the hardware and software architecture, components, modules, interfaces, and data processing units for a computer system to satisfy specified requirement specification. In other words, design may be referred as system decomposition into modules and relationships between the modules. Design of the information processing system covers the activities of determining detailed requirements, design of data/ information flow, design of database, design of user interface, physical design, and design of hardware/ software configuration. The designing activities in SDLC result into a blueprint of the system/software architecture as per the give specifications.

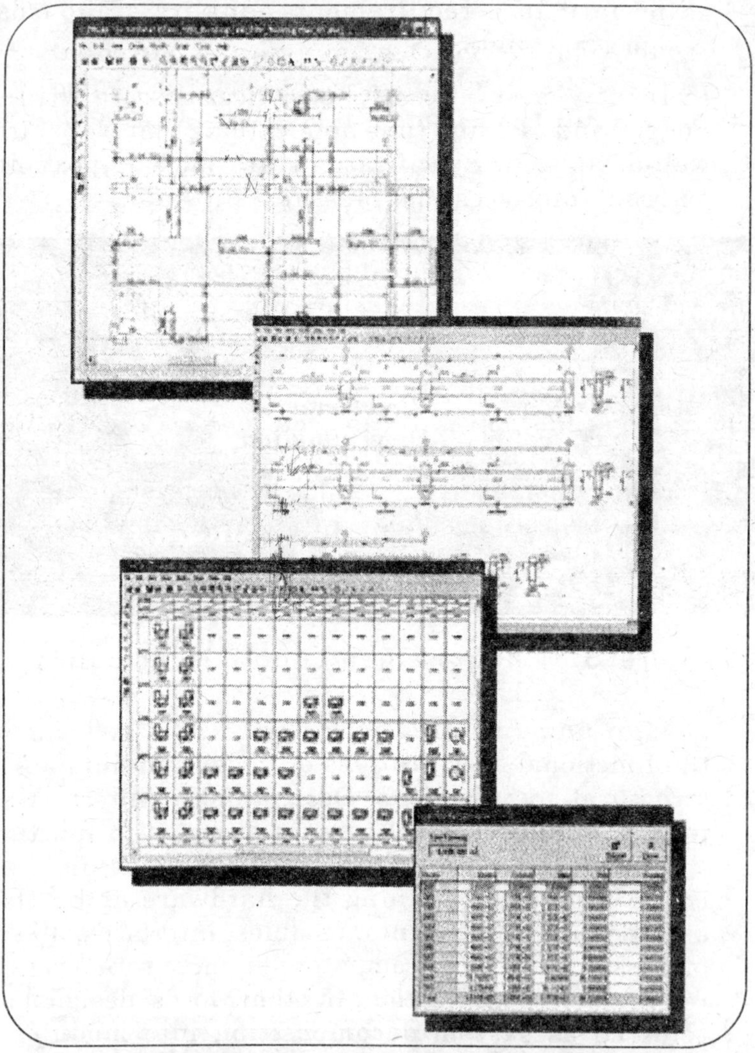

Figure 3.4: designing structure of software

- **Coding:** Coding activity is often known as "Programming'. Reducing a design to a computer program may be the most obvious part of the software engineering job. In this phase of SDLC, the program codes are written for implementation of the algorithms and designs into the high level or low level programming languages. Coding defines the entire layout of the programs including headers of comments, definitions of constants, naming conventions for identifiers and labels and subprograms, structuring the program and its control. The goal of coding is to implement the design in a programming language in a maintainable and controllable manner. The coding activity starts after some designing has been completed and the complete and unambiguous details of the components under development are given. Coding is then done for the modules and their interfaces to enable the system to perform its task.

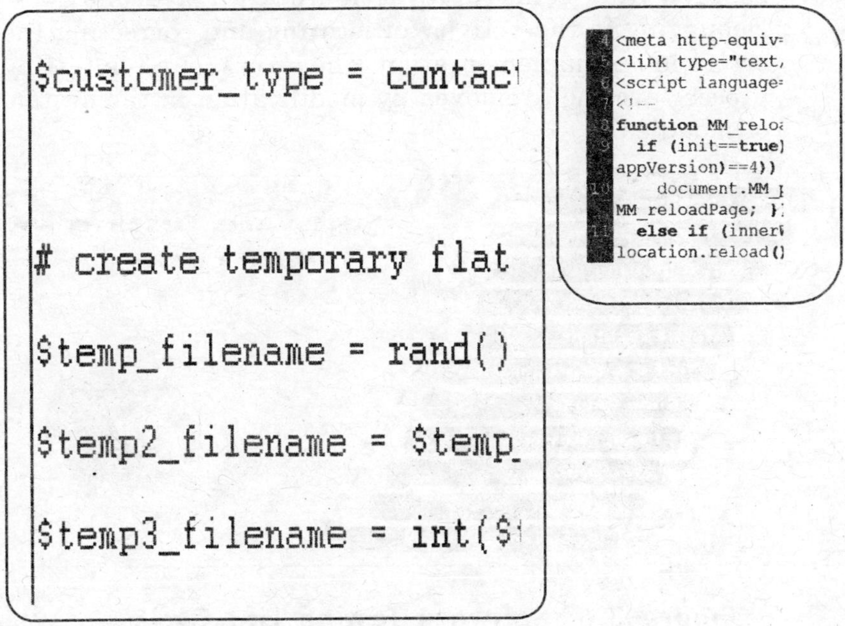

Figure 3.5: Coding & Programming

- **Testing & Debugging:** After implementation, testing of the system is an important step in SDLC. It is an expensive step and consumes thirty to fifty percent of the cost of development. Testing is the process of finding errors introduced in any stage of development. Although, each and every step is carried out with immense care and checks, yet some of the errors in the system remain left unresolved. Testing is the process of executing the software with an intension of finding an error in it. It should be noted here that testing can show the presence of an error but it cannot certify the absence of error. This is because of the fact that a complete and vigorous testing for each and every probable input value is not possible.

The testing process generates symptoms of failure of the system for presence of some error. After catching these symptoms, next step is to locate the place where the error resides and remove it with appropriate changes. Debugging is the activity of locating and correcting the errors in the implementation. The errors found in testing process are then removed by modification in the system or modules.

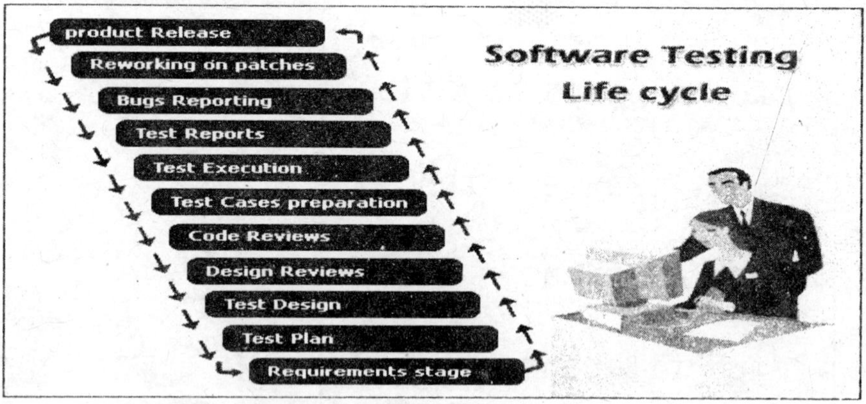

Figure 3.6: Software Testing Life Cycle

- **Documentation:** An important (and often overlooked) task is documenting the internal design of software for the purpose of future maintenance and enhancement. Documentation is most important for external interfaces. Software Documentation is written text that accompanies computer software. It either explains how it operates or how to use it. In fact, the term software documentation means different things to different people. This article describes the term as used by the largest groups of users. In fact, the documentation is required during and after each phase of development including planning, analyzing, designing, coding, testing and even after release of the product. It is to make the process repeatable and traceable. These documents will in future be used for studying the success or failure of process or parts of process. The documents are also used to analyze the strong and weak parts of the process. In this manner, the documentation is important not only for the product but also for the process.

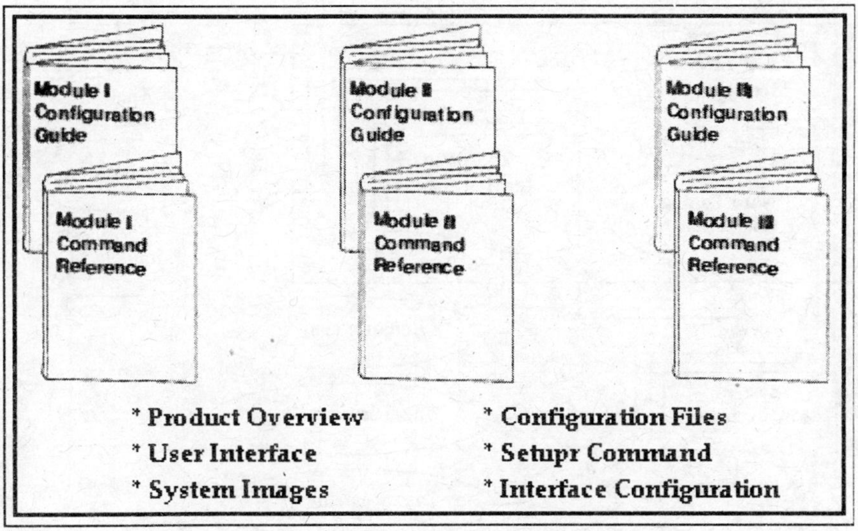

Figure 3.7: Documentation

- **Maintenance:** Software maintenance is one of the activities in software engineering, and is the process of enhancing and optimizing deployed software as well as remedying defects. Maintaining and enhancing software to cope with newly discovered problems or new requirements can take far more time than the initial development of the software. Not only may it be necessary to add code that does not fit the original design but just determining how software works at some point after it is completed may require significant effort by a software engineer. About 2/3 of all software engineering work is maintenance, but this statistic can be misleading. A small part of that is fixing bugs. Most maintenance is extending systems to do new things, which in many ways can be considered new work. Similarly, about 2/3 of all civil engineering, architecture, and construction work is maintenance in a similar way.

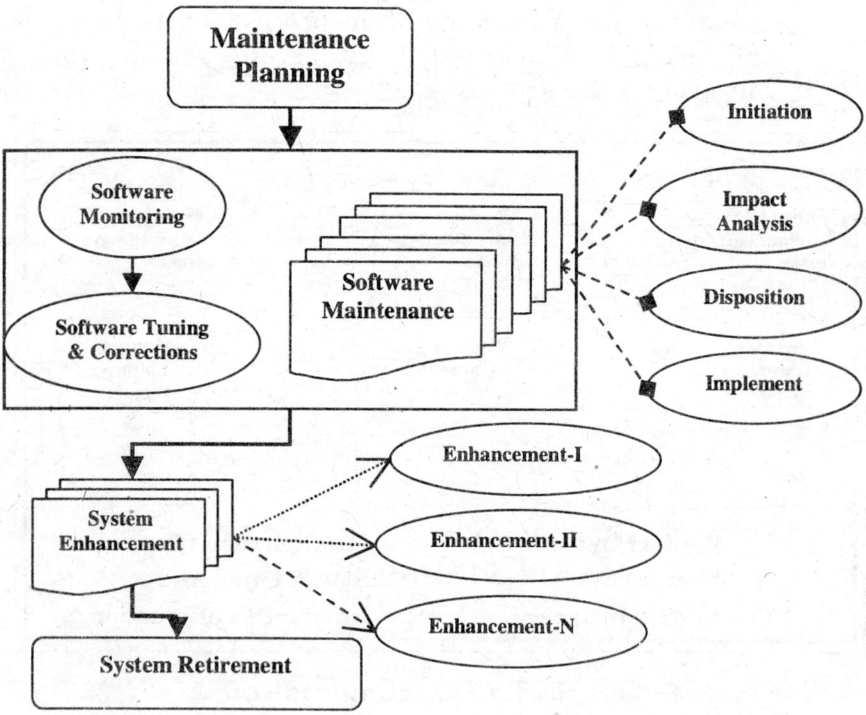

Figure 3.8: Software Maintenance Life Cycle

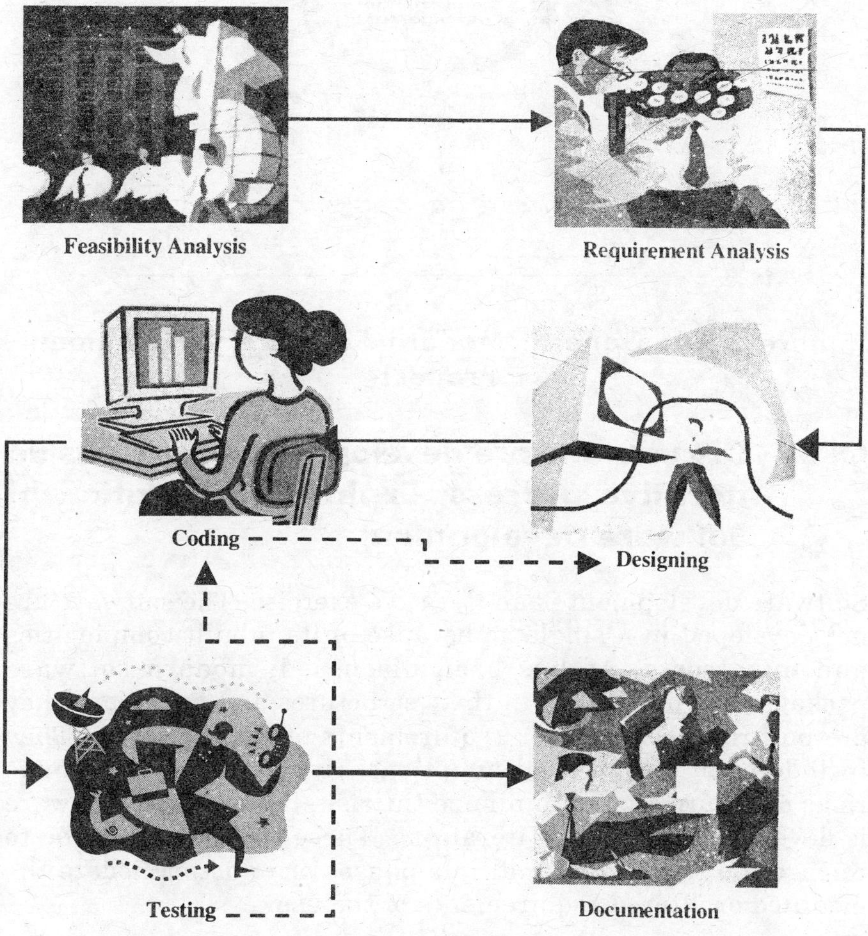

Figure 3.9: General Linear Software Development Process

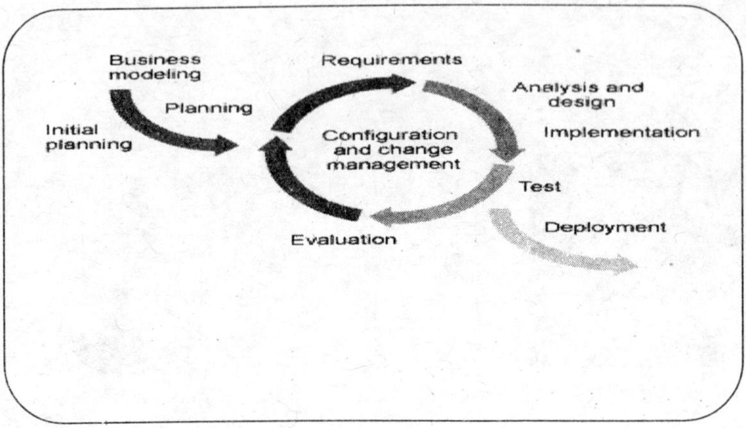

Figure 3.10: General Modern Software Development Process

Q. 3. Discuss software development process as an iterative process. Explain an iteration of Software Development.

Software development is an iterative exercise. The software are not developed in a single go because of its inbuilt complexities and huge costs. As has been discussed, modern software packages are not simple in their structures and behavior. They are built to meet complex requirements of the consumer. They include huge resource consumptions. Hence they involve huge risks of failure too. To minimize the risk, the complete software is developed in multiple iterations. These iterations may be to release the software in multiple phases or to accommodate the modified or altered requirements of the use.

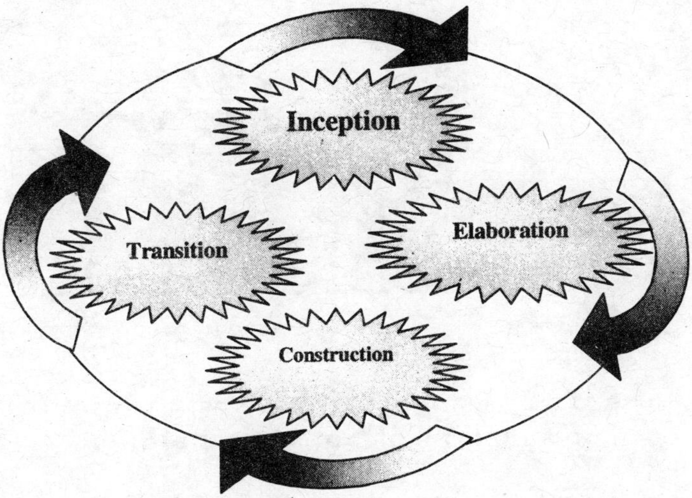

Figure 3.11: Iteration Phases in Software Development Life Cycle

Each of the iterations of software development is executed in four phase: Inception, Elaboration, Construction and Transition. The inception phase of the iteration is dedicated to incept the idea of development, understanding the requirements, performing feasibility study and describing the scope and size of the project. The elaboration phase leads to elaborate the involved risk in the process and the product of development. In this phase, risk is evaluated; a formal project plan is developed and baseline architecture of the development is established. In the construction phase, the actual implementation of the plan is executed and the software is implemented with programming languages on its required platform as per its specified environment and the outcomes are compared and tested against their specifications. Construction phase involves the use of different development, testing and debugging tools. In the transition phase, the iteration transition is drafted according to the feedback of the consumer and customer about the results of construction phase. The transitions phase is focused for complete customer satisfaction and achievement of the product.

Figure 3.12: Estimated Phase wise Resource Consumption of Software Iteration

Q. 4. Describe Inception phase of Software process iteration.

Any software process iteration starts with inception phase that is important for planning for the process and product of the iteration. Inception may be considered as the smallest phase in the project. Inception phase is dedicated to requirement gathering for the product and outlining the goals of the process. The outcomes of this phase specify expectations of the consumer and customer from the developed system. The inception phase is focused towards the following goals:

- To describe the initial requirements
- To establish a business case for the project
- To establish the project scope and boundary conditions
- To identify the people, organizations, external systems that will interact with your system and key requirements that will drive the design tradeoffs
- To outline one or more candidate architectures
- To set milestones of the project and constraints incurred.
- To identify risks and estimating costs, durations and schedules for the process and iteration

Q. 5. Discuss focus and activities involved in Elaboration phase of Software process iteration.

The elaboration phase is primarily focused for

i. assessment of the involved risk in the process of development,

ii. for addressing different factors of risk and

iii. for establishment of a reliable and efficient architecture of the system.

Figure 3.13: Elaboration

The activities of elaboration phase give a logical and conceptual base to the estimations of schedule and cost of the development made in the inception phase.

The final Elaboration phase deliverable is a formal guideline or a plan (including cost and schedule estimates) for the Construction phase.

The primary goals of this phase include the following:

- To elaborate the nonfunctional requirements of the system
- To produce a proven, architectural baseline for the software system

- To produce a detailed and revised description of involved risk of failure and to eliminate the highly-disastrous risks of the project
- To ensure that the critical tools, processes, standards, and guidelines have been put in place for the Construction phase

Q. 6. What are different types of risks to be addressed during Elaboration phase of Software process iteration?

Tomorrow's problem is today's risk. Software risk is a probability of future encounter with a cause of loss or failure of the software project. There may be a risk o cost overshoot, schedule mismanagement, bad performance or software failure while maintenance. Risk may be of development of some wrong functionality or component or losing focus in changing and accommodating user's diversified requirements. Some other risks may be about the performance, quality and worth of the software. Sales and marketing of the software also face many other risks.

Primarily, risks may be categorized into the following categories:

i. Requirements Risks

ii. Technological Risks

iii. Skills Risks

iv. Political Risks

Q. 7. Discuss how the different types of risks may be dealt in elaboration phase.

In the elaboration phase, different types of risks are addressed and dealt as risk management. Although, different types of risks are dealt in their own ways according to their nature of occurrence and degree of consequences yet, by following some guidelines, different common types of risks may be avoided or minimized in most of the software projects. A few of these guidelines are discussed here:

i. Dealing with Requirements Risks

- Use cases can be employed to provide basis for communication between customer and developers in planning a project. Use-case is a typical interaction between user and system to achieve a goal. E.g. as we use ATM one use case will be - Dispense cash, another may be print receipt, display balance and so on.
- Skeleton Domain models can be drawn using OO techniques like UML
- Considerations for Workflow, Rulebase, Security need to made

ii. Dealing with Technological Risks

- Build prototypes that try out pieces of technology that we plan to use. e.g. if we are using Java and relational database, build a simple application using these.
- Try out tools that support our choice of technology. Spend time getting comfortable with them.
- Try releasing the software in multiple versions.
- Also, consider how easy or difficult it is to port to other platforms in future.

iii. Dealing with Skills Risks

- Acquire skills through training and mentoring
- Read relevant technical books
- Look for patterns
    - ❑ Pattern is an idea that has been useful in one practical context and may probably be useful in others
    - ❑ In the modeling context, they can be looked upon as example models
    - ❑ They describe common ways of doing things

- They are collected by people who spot repeating themes in analysis and design
- Each theme is described so that people can read it and see how to apply it. Thus, patterns promote reuse.

iii. Dealing with Political Risks

- Training on Effective Team work can be of great help here.
- The cost and schedule estimates can be comfortably made at this stage and create a plan for construction.

Q. 8. Describe construction phase of Software process iteration and its activities.

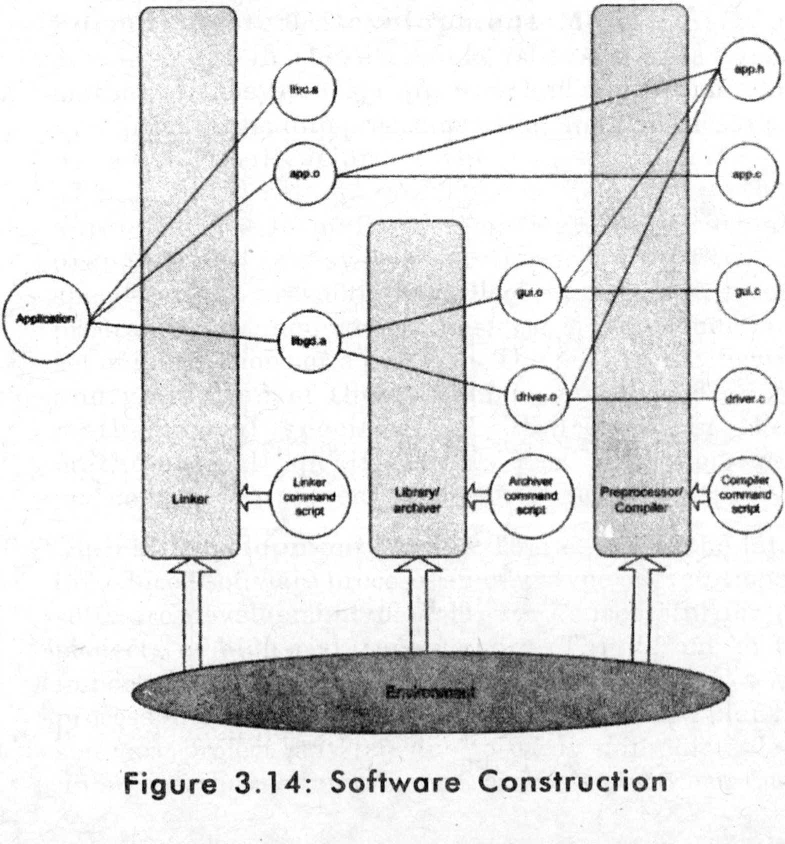

Figure 3.14: Software Construction

Construction is the largest phase in the project. In this phase all the components of the system are built and integrated on the foundation laid in Elaboration phase. Each iteration results in an executable release of the software. All the components and features are tested thoroughly in the construction phase and debugged for the errors caught. This phase is responsible for producing quality products under managed resources and optimized costs in finitely defined schedules. Finishing the construction phase leads to the producing of an actual stable product that is mature enough for a formal release and acceptable when compared with the planned system.

List of objectives of this phase include the following:

- To flesh out the design of the system and design modeling
- To ensure that the system meets the needs of its users and expectations of the developers and managers
- To implement the component-units and testing each unit
- To integrate the develop units into the complete system and testing of the software product
- To write the software documentation and manuals as expected
- To minimize development costs by optimizing resources and maintaining the expected quality and schedules of development.
- To develop useful versions of your system

Q. 9. Explain activities of Transition phase of Software process iteration. What is the focus of this phase?

The final phase in iteration in the project development life cycle is the Transition phase. This phase is focused towards a successful releasing of the software product. Transition phase ends with a formal handing over the software product to the user or the costumer. In this phase the system is deployed to the target users. Feedback received from an initial release or versions of the software may result in further enhancements or alterations in the software over the course of multiple iterations. The Transition phase also includes planning of the development of new releases, correction of defects in the system, conversions or optimization of the software, conversion of operational databases, marketing and user training.

Figure 3.15: The Transition Phase

List of objectives and activities of this phase include the following:

- Conversion of operational database and User Training
- Rolling out the product to sales and marketing
- Customer satisfaction and alterations in the system as per the feedback of the consumer.
- Achievement of the concurrence of the stakeholder that the product expectations are met stable and consistently with acceptability standards.
- Developing the report of the complete iteration and concluding for the factors of success and failures.
- Planning for the next iteration of production.
- Planning the enhancement of the system

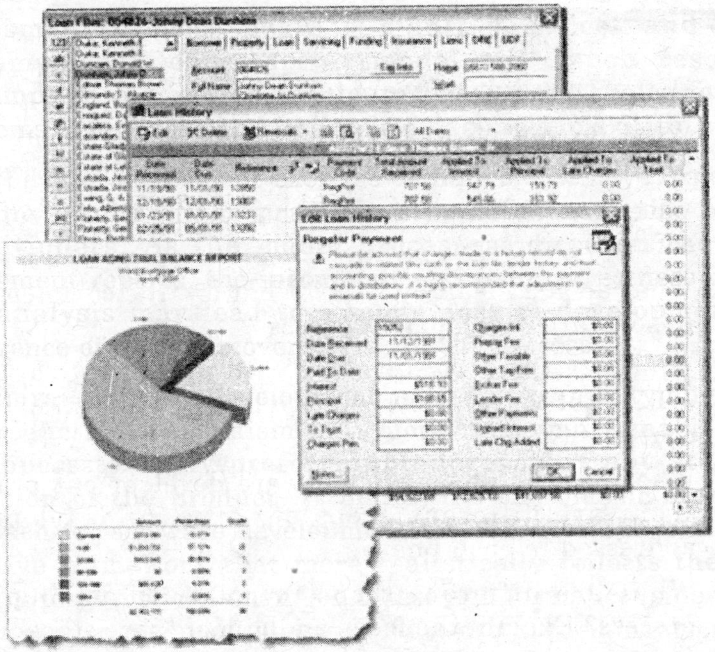

Figure 3.16: Iteration transition in Software

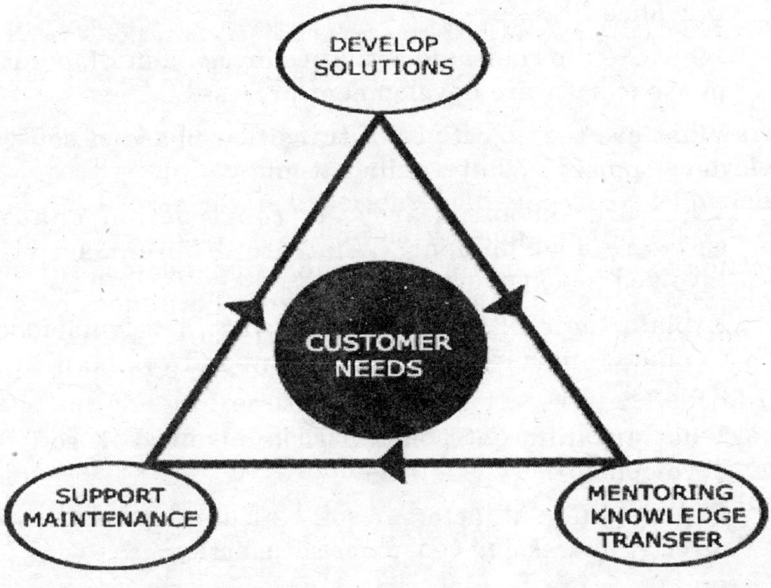

Figure 3.17: Meeting customer's needs in iterations

Exercises

i. Define the term software process.

ii. What do you mean by Key Process Area (KPA)? What are different KPA's in software development process?

iii. What are the important factor affecting the success of a software process?

iv. What do you mean by Risk? What are the common risks in software development process?

v. What are the risks involved with sales and marketing of the software? How can such risk be minimized or controlled?

vi. What are the phases in software development process? What are different areas of software development addressed in each phase?

vii. What are different steps in software development process? Explain the focus and aim of these steps?

viii. What is the goal of inception phase in software development? What are different activities involved in this phase?

ix. What are the goals and activities involved in Elaboration phase of software development process?

x. What are the objectives of transition phase of software development? What are its outputs?

xi. What are the focus areas of construction phase of software development? What are different activities involved in construction phase?

xii. Explain the risk involved in software development due to change in hardware technology and communication devices?

xiii. What are different political risks involved in software development?

xiv. Explain different factors in software development process directly addressing consumer satisfaction.

xv. What do you mean by risk management?

4

Software Process Models

Managing the lifecycle of a software system is a complex task. In software engineering, many attempts have been made to define and achieve the general process of software development in an abstraction. These abstractions are required to make the software development process easy and more understandable. Modeling the process makes the process easy to follow and leads to a traceable success.

The software development process is defined as a framework of application of methodologies to develop reliable software. But the general description of the software process is not adoptable and acceptable for all types of problems and development in hand. Different conditions, different objectives, different sizes and different complexities of the system under development need different types of abstractions of the general process that focuses of different characteristics of the product and the process.

Things in software development are not as straight forward as shown in the general process some or as depicted in some traditional models. It is a challenging and complex task containing many factor of success.

The effort of specifying and adopting the right model of a development process provides the advantages of better quality, time and cost planning and good customer satisfaction. A common formal basis will enable the easy exchange of specific process models between interested parties.

Q. 1. What is Software process model?

A *model* is an abstract representation of a system (real or imaginary) that enables us to answer questions about the system. Models are constructed of the problem domain in order to understand the problem and solution domain in order to understand different solutions and trade-offs.

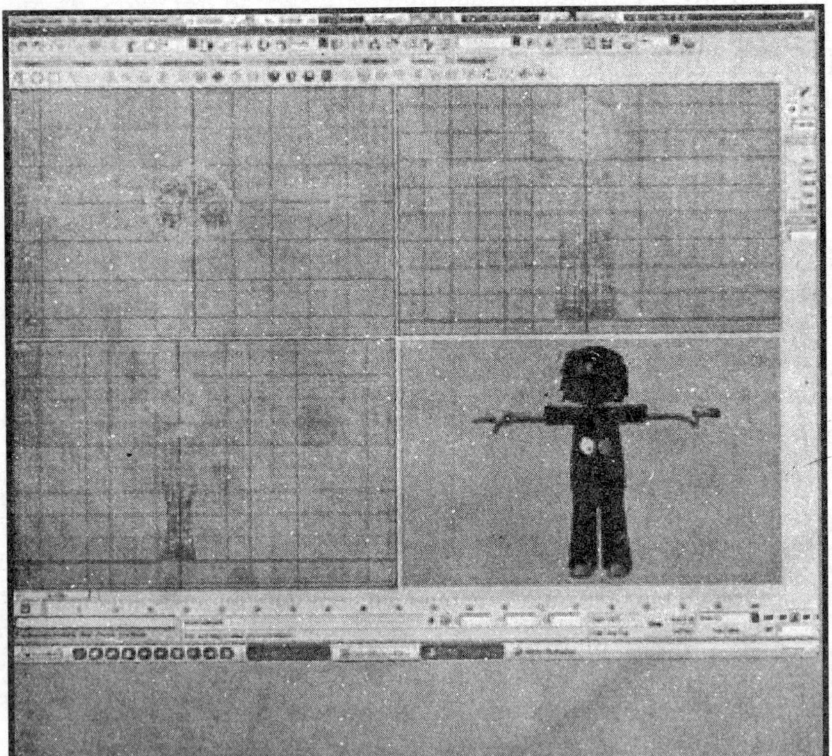

Figure 4.1: The Modeling

Software Process Model is one specific embodiment of a software process. It is an abstract representation for a software development life cycle (SDLC) and sometimes also called

Software Development Life Cycle Model (SDLC Model). A process model specifies a general purpose in the form of a set of stages in which the complete project or the process is suggested to be divided. The process model also includes the domain & range of the products of each step and constraints of execution of each step in the model.

Q. 2. What are the desired characteristics of software development process model?

Desired characteristics of a software process model can be listed as below:

1. **Defined:** The model should be clearly defined with all its steps of execution, their need and importance in the process, their inputs and output products, people involved in the step, constraints and limitations. Each step should be clearly described with its intensions of execution and focus of the tasks involved in it.

2. **Predictability:** The model should be able to predict the output of each step and its usefulness quiet early in the process before it actually completes. The model should be able to give an estimation of the cost and time for development of the product before building it. A good model provides a practical time schedule for milestones in the development process. It predicts the quality and risks of failure of the project.

3. **Continuity of process:** The model is expected to represent a continuous and natural flow of activities of software development. For example, system analysis is required before an engineer design the system and testing is done after some system is implemented. Software development is a continuous process consisting of many sequential and concurrent activities. These activities should be incorporated in the model with their retained continuity and sequence.

4. **Communication:** A good process *facilitates* communications. It provides channels between the parties that need to communicate, and indicates the

form, purpose and goal of each communication. Not only this, it also defines the role of each communicating party in the interest of work product.

5. **Iterations and Consistency:** Software development is an iterative task. Iterations allow the developers to take advantage of what was learned in the previous stages of development or during the development of earlier versions of the system. The iteration allows re-planning and re-implementation of a task for better results. The process model should be able to accommodate the needs of multiple iterations in the development life cycle.

6. **Quantification & Controllability:** The model should represent the development process in a controllable manner. Generally, it is believed that a quantifiable thing is more controllable than a non quantifiable entity. Hence, it is recommended to get a quantifiable process than can describe the development progress, its cost & time consumptions, resource requirements, quality constraints etc. in a measurable format. The best way to control a software project is to continuously measure its progress, compare the progress against the plan, and adjust the development parameters to correct any deviation from the plan.

7. **Testability:** The model should support the testability of the product. The model should be able to give a formal and strong base and infrastructure to provide reasonable testing and hence should reduce the efforts and cost of testing the product.

8. **Maintainability:** The software development process model should provide a maintainable control over the modifications made in the product with intensions of enhancement of functionality or technology of the product. A formal plan for the maintenance activities should be defined in the process model.

9. **Simplicity & Effectiveness:** The process model is expected to implement the process in an effective, simple and acceptable manner. Too complex models are not

expected to be effective in the team and tend to fail. The model should be natural in the process and give expected results in the product in terms of functionality, quality, time, cost and efforts.

10 **Generality:** The model should be defined in a way that is applicable to development of solutions to the most general problems. The model should not be dedicated to a particular problem or a particular category of problems.

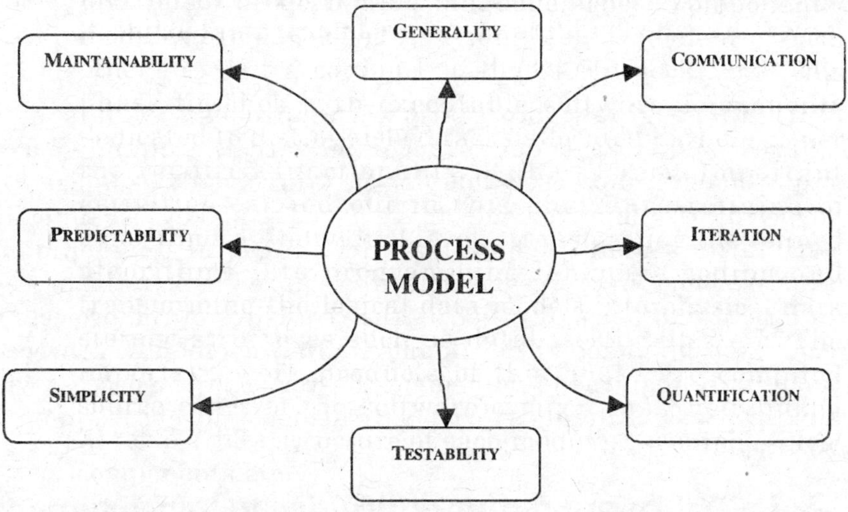

Figure 4.2: Common Characteristics of Process Model

Q. 3. Why continuous improvements are required in process models?

Improvements in products are not the only focus of software engineering but enhancements and improvements in development process models is another major focus of software engineering practices. These improvements are required for accommodating the changing user requirements, technology up-gradations and the increased complexities in software specifications. With due course of time, as the hardware technologies and network technologies change, traditional processes need to be enhanced to accommodate these changes.

Traditionally, the developed systems were not such complex and large as they are in current scenario. Earlier, the software systems were based on a small set of functionalities to process a set of simple data with an intension of automation or control of some regular tasks. Slowly, the expectations of users extended to enhance the usage of software systems for much complex automations and controls and the software development went complex and challenging. The development processes went consuming huge costs and time periods. Practitioners then needed more formal processes and practices for estimating schedules and budgets of development, implementation and maintenance of the system.

With increasing complexities, the process models need improvements in them to accommodate the changed user requirements, increased complexities, involved risks, size and involved cost. Improvements are required to make close to reality estimations about schedules and budget of development. Improvements in process models are required to plan the process in formal manner and to set up the requisites of the projects at each step or phase of development. Improvements in process models are required to implement controls over the process with flexibilities in changes in specifications and environmental constraints.

Q. 4. What are major difficulties in improvements in software development process models?

Need to improve the process models is quite obvious but improving process models face many difficulties. Improvement in process models need more serious and sincere efforts and demand long researches and observations of success and failure histories of the process. Industries generally do not pay much attentions and efforts or it may be said that industries are not serious to invest time and resources for such activities. Another major difficulty faced in improvement of process models if lack of knowledge about the traditional and modern formal practices in the domain. Practitioners and professional developers generally give more importance to the practical works of development rather investing time in literature survey or experimenting. They work under time pressures and pay almost no attention in improving the work strategies. They lack in familiarities with available best approaches and follow the common approach that they had been following in history and they feel themselves comfortable with rather than trying a new one. Another important difficulty may be the psychological nature of reluctance to changes. Generally, industries do not accept any change in process as they feel it to be a breach in control powers of managements or flexibilities of developers. Both ways, the industry avoid trying working with a new process.

Q. 5. Discuss major types of S/W process models.

Software process model are the abstract models of software development process addressing some general problems of software development. Software Process Model is one specific embodiment of a software process. It is an abstract representation for a software development life cycle (SDLC) and sometimes also called Software Development Life Cycle Model (SDLC Model). Software development organizations have been facing complexities of their profession and need of continuously improving the models of the processes. Many organizations have been putting continuous efforts in formalizing software development procedure and improving these development processes. Long history of these efforts has evolved with many process models important to be discussed here.

- **Build & Fix (Ad-hoc) Model:** The earliest known development process that is also known as quick-fix model. This approach constructs the software without a formal specification or design. Instead of designing, the team simply builds the product and reworks as many times as required. This development process is based on a hit & trial approach in which the developer or the members of developing team try to write the software on the basis of their experience of development. After writing the software, it is checked for its functionality to meet the expectations. Found errors are corrected and the new build is again carried through the same procedure till the software is verified satisfactory to the expectations of the consumer. This may be a good, quick and cost effective process for very small projects that do not need often modifications or maintenance.

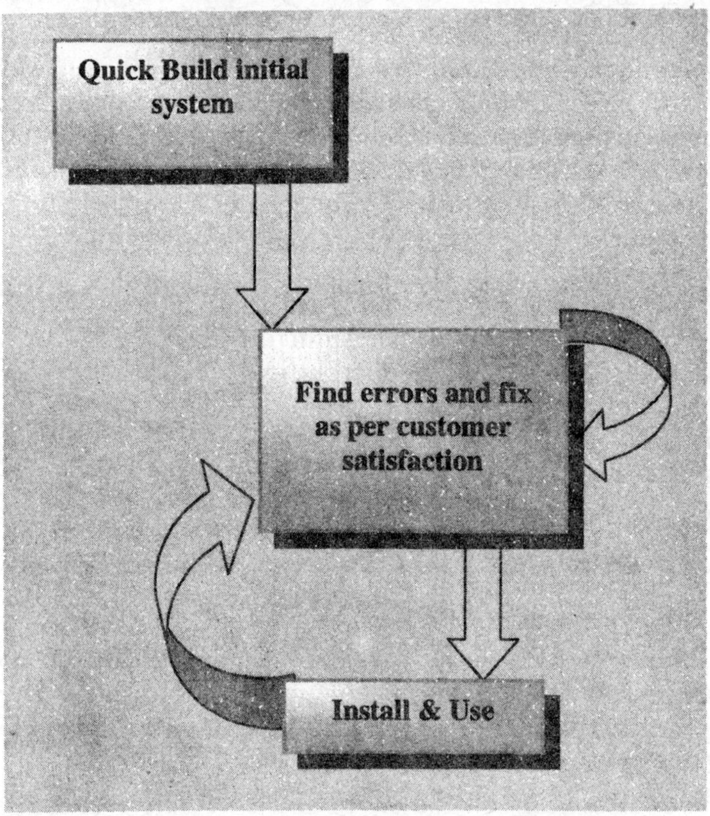

Figure 4.3: Build & Fix Model

- **Waterfall Model:** This model is proposed by Royce as a sequential series of steps of software development process. Waterfall model is taken as the simplest software process model that follows a non iterative acyclic procedure in order to produce the desired software product. The model follows a big bang approach in which the complete software is delivered at the end of the process in a single version. The process may be described as shown in Figure 4.4. In this model, the steps of software development include requirement analysis, designing, detailed designing, unit implementation, unit testing, integration of tested modules, system testing, installation, operation and maintenance. All these activities are performed in a defined sequential order without skipping. None of the activity can be revised once has been closed and passes the results to the next step for use. Hence the complete process runs as a waterfall that cannot skip any point in fall nor can repeat to any point once traversed.

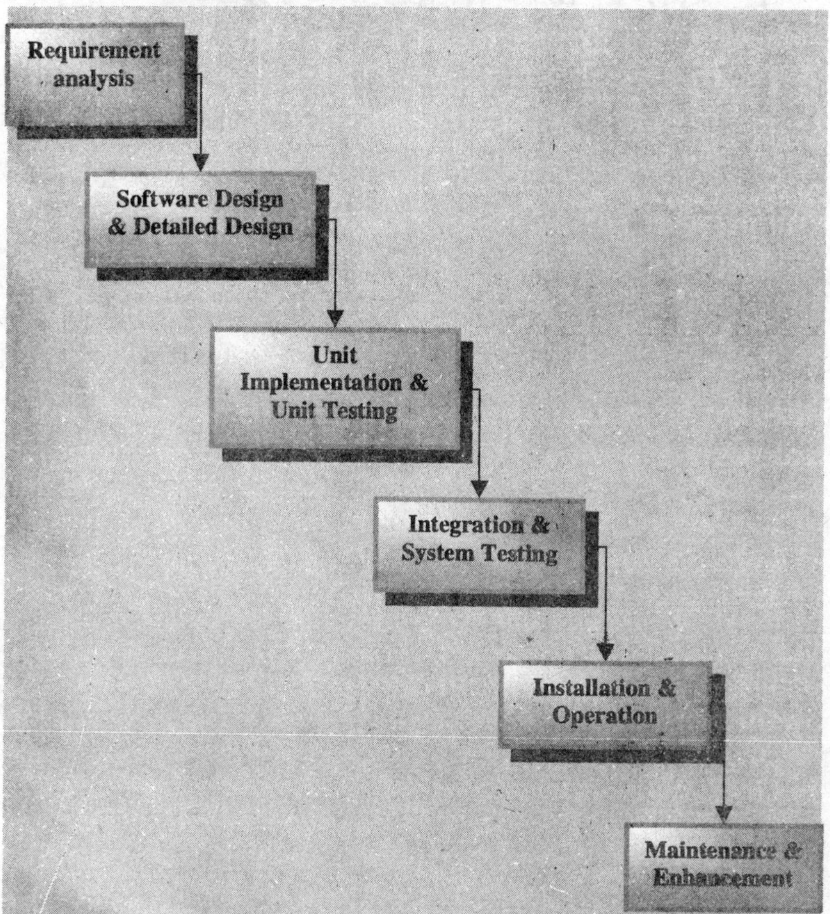

Figure 4.4: Waterfall Model

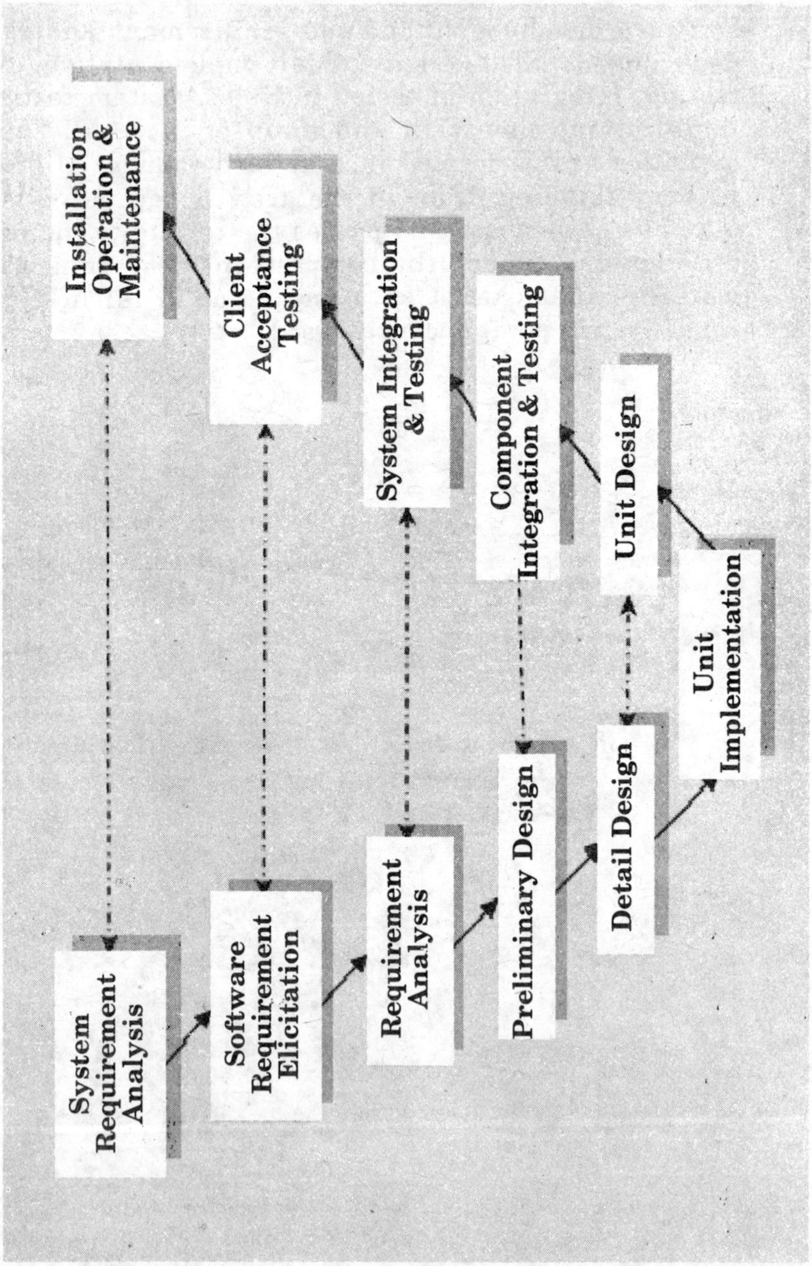

Figure 4.5: V-Shape Model

- **V-Shape Model:** This model also describes the process about constructing the application complete at a time, same as in the waterfall model, without feedback between the steps of construction. This model is strictly focused of testability of each step in the development cycle. It gives equal focuses on testing rather than treating it as an afterthought. Each step generates a test plan for it which is used ate different levels if testing as shown in the figure 4.5. Hence V-shape model supports parallel testing for each development phase. It encapsulates the steps in verification and validation phases for each step in SDLC. This model shows the typical sequence of development activities on the left hand side downfall series and the corresponding sequence of test activities on the right hand side upraise series, as shown in Figure 4.5.

- **Evolutionary Development Model:** This model is based on the idea of developing an initial incomplete unstructured implementation and exposing it to the user for evaluation, gathering the comments and refining the product through a number of iterations till the consumer expectations are met. The process iterates the activities of software specification, designing, implementation and validation. Objective of this model is to work with the customer and understand his expectations and requirement in depth. This mode of development is followed in the projects where user's requirements are not understandable and comprehensible. The system development starts with the components those are well understood and ambiguous components are created with discussion with the customer and reviews of the consumers.

- **Prototype Model:** This model is one of the most commonly followed process model, a type of evolutionary development. The basic idea of this model is to develop a dummy working model of the system before its actual development in order to ensure confidence in accuracy of the software specifications with modest consultancy with the customer. In this model, the vague specifications are quickly designed and developed into a trial product and produced to the consumer for evaluation. The specifications are refined as per the feedback and reconverted into another prototype. The process is repeated till freezing the specifications consistent with fulfillment of consumer expectations. The finally freeze specifications are then developed into the deliverable product. The model is depicted as below in the Figure 4.6.

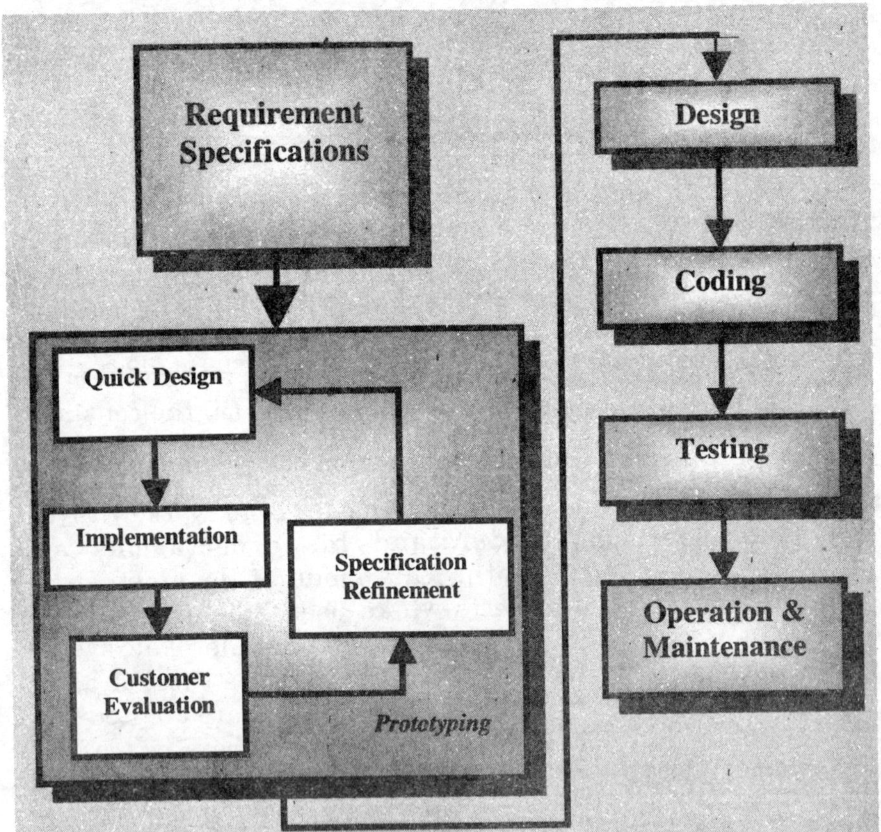

Figure 4.6: Prototype SDLC Model

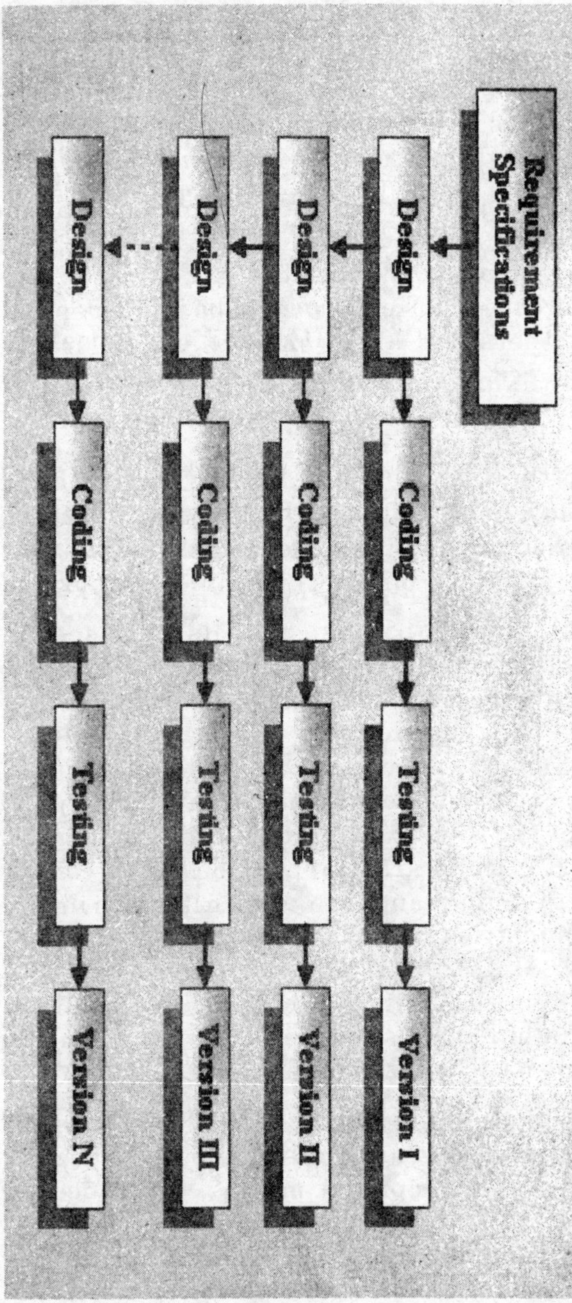

Figure 4.7: Iterative Incremental Enhancement Model

- **Incremental Enhancement Model:** This is commonly followed process model especially introduced for huge projects that are completed in multiple phases of delivery i.e. multiple versions of the products are produced in the course of completely meeting the consumer requirements. The model starts with a big problem statement that is described with a list of requirement specification in an order of priority/risk. The specifications high in the preference list are planned to be implemented first before the others and an incomplete but desirable system is developed in the first iteration of the development cycle. The lower preference specifications are added in multiple subsequent versions. This model provides a better control over the big projects allowing better budgeting and management. The model at a glance may be drawn as follows in Figure 4.7.

- **Formal System Development Model:** Software development in these models is based on a formal mathematical system specification and transformation of this specification into programs using mathematical tools. Also the verification of the system is based on mathematical arguments. This means that in these approaches, a formal mathematical specification is prepared for the system and these mathematical specifications are mapped to logical components of a programming language to transform it into a functional set of instructions or a program. The testing, verification and validation of the system is also based on the mathematical specification. Hence, again these mathematical specifications are validated with mathematical arguments.

- **Spiral Development Model:** This is one of the latest introduced software process, another type of evolutionary software development models, very successful for the projects of high risk involvement. This is one of the important models which incorporate project-risks and process uncertainties in formal discussions and plans. A software project may fail due to many unpredictable or unforeseen happenings. Hence, project risk becomes very important factor to be included in development process and plans. As shown in Figure 4.8, Spiral model splits the development process into four major segments viz. planning, risk analysis, development/implementation and assessment/evaluation. These four sectors are iterated through out the development cycle to produce the quality products.

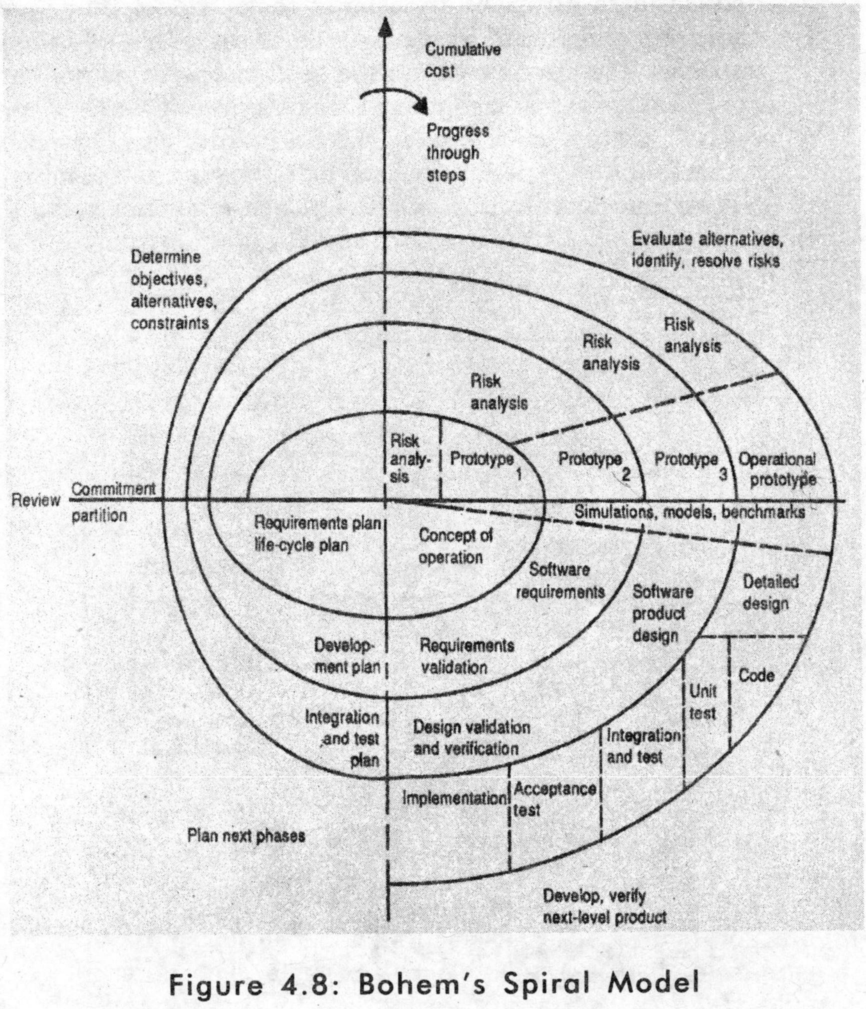

Figure 4.8: Bohem's Spiral Model

- **Reused Base Development Model:** Reusable component based development is a newer approach and is based on component-level assembly of existing reusable software components. This model exercises on the basis of significant number of existing reusable components that may be integrated into a big system to achieve the desired functionality. The approach works upon selection of required existing software components dedicated to different functional tasks, development of required additional modules and integration of these modules. The integrated system is then tested as per the specifications. Reuse based development encourage active usage of CAD & CASE tools and special techniques to speed up analysis, design, assembly, testing and installation in order to achieve quick results.

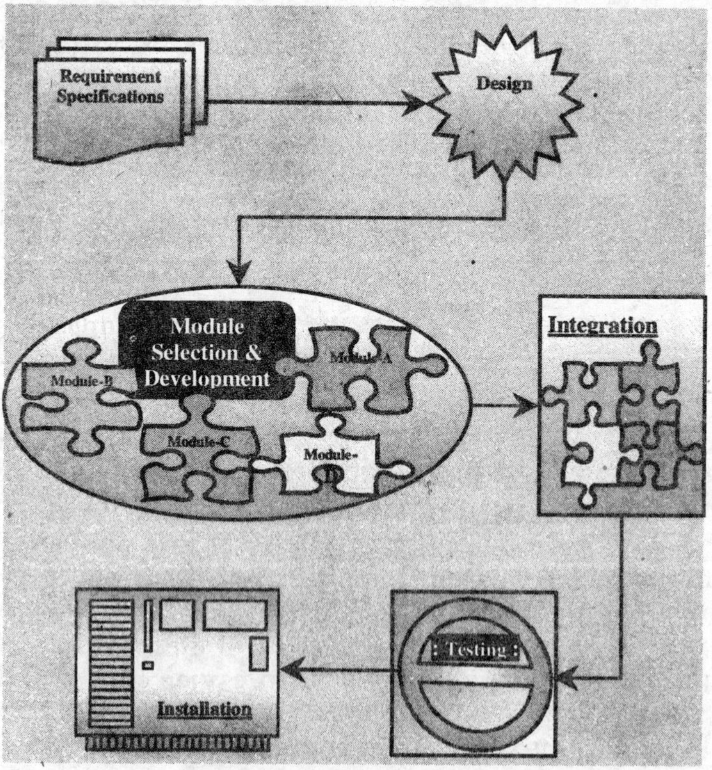

Figure 4.9: RAD Process Model

Q. 6. Explain Waterfall process model of SDLC. State its work-products at each step of process.

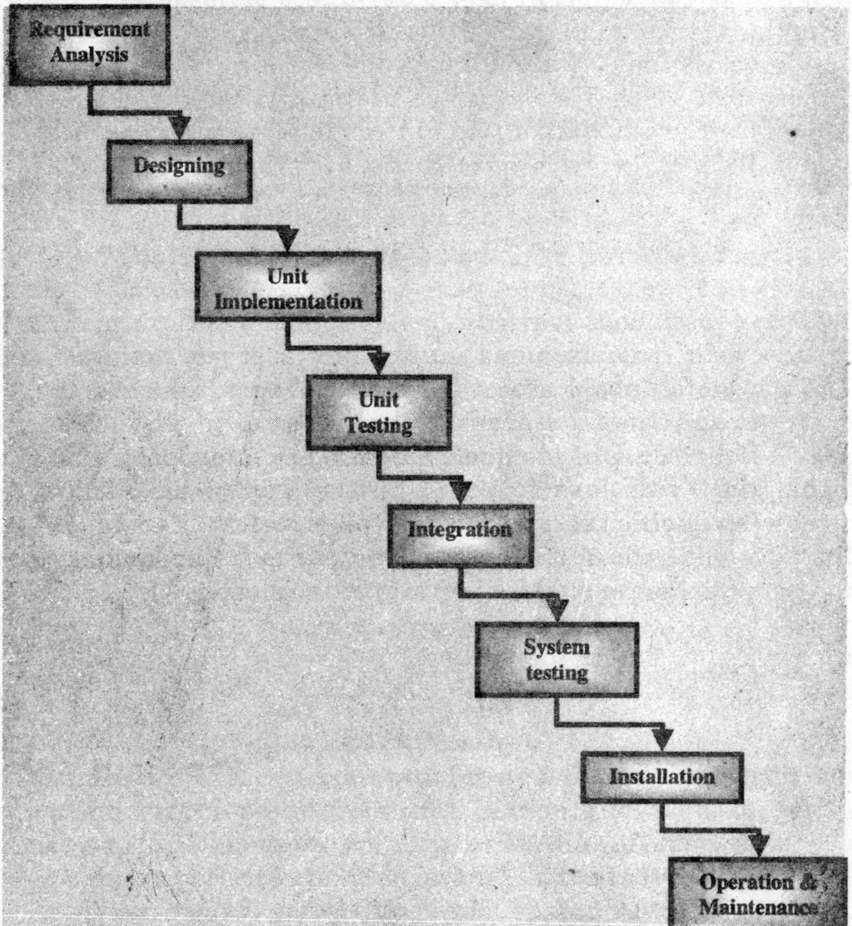

Figure 4.10: Waterfall Process Model

Waterfall model follows a number of development steps in a defined order in a non iterative manner to develop the desired software product. In this model, the completed software is produced in the end of the process in a single version. The process may be depicted as shown below in Figure 4.10. The process is structured as a cascading of phases in the development cycle. Each phase is structured into a set of activities dedicated to a specific goal of the phase. The activities involved in the waterfall model are discussed here.

- **Requirement Analysis:** The goal of this phase is to understand the customer needs and expectations. This phase is dedicated to identify and explore the required qualities of the system to be developed. This step defines ***'what'*** should be included in the software irrespective and independent of ***'how'*** these requirements are achieved. Major activities of this phase include defining the system, compiling problem statement and requirement definitions, establishing milestones and project schedule, validating system specifications and justifying practical feasibility of the development. The system service limitations, efficiency expectations, interfacing requirements and other work product goals are established during this phase by the software developing team in consultations with the customer. The work product of this step comes out as a document known as Software Requirements Specification.

- **Designing:** Designing phase is focused for creating a blueprint for the implementation of the software system. The goal of the designing phase is to convert SRS document into a structural architecture for software components and their relationships and communication channels (interfaces) at different levels of abstraction. In this phase, different software modules and functional units are identified that will cover requirements specified in SRS document, distinguished tasks are assigned to these functional units, they are organized over a common platform where they are made capable to communicate with each other to access their services. Important activities involved in this phase are designing the system deployment structure, designing logical data models for different components, designing algorithmic structure for functional units and validating the architecture and algorithms to synthesize the individual component and component interfaces. Some suitable CAD tools may also be used for these activities. The work products of the designing phase are system deployment design model, logical data model, algorithmic (or pseudo code) design of functional units and document of detailed design decisions.

- **Unit Implementation:** Once the designing of the software components is finished, these components are implemented in some selected high level (sometimes low level also) programming language. These components/ modules are developed individually independent of each other in strict accordance of the design document. This phase finishes with executable software components dedicated to distinguished tasks allocated to them as per the required functionality of the system. Important activities carried out in this phase are refining of algorithms at individual levels, transforming the refined algorithms into programming language coding and transforming the logical data models into physical data storage structures such as databases or files etc. The important work products of this phase are compiled source codes of the software components, their linked libraries, data structure of each module, executable files/ components etc.

- **Unit Testing:** This phase of process model is dedicated to testing of the developed modules/components of the software. The modules prepared in the last phase are tested and validated in this phase by a team of experts. These modules are validated for their functional correctness, reliability and closeness to the specification. A formal test plan is used as a base for validation. Required changes are made in the modules to remove errors in them. The irremovable errors are documented and precautionary actions are proposed in the same document. Major work products of this activity are formal test plan for individual modules, test case execution result documentation (logs of test cases) and proposed precautions while executing the module.

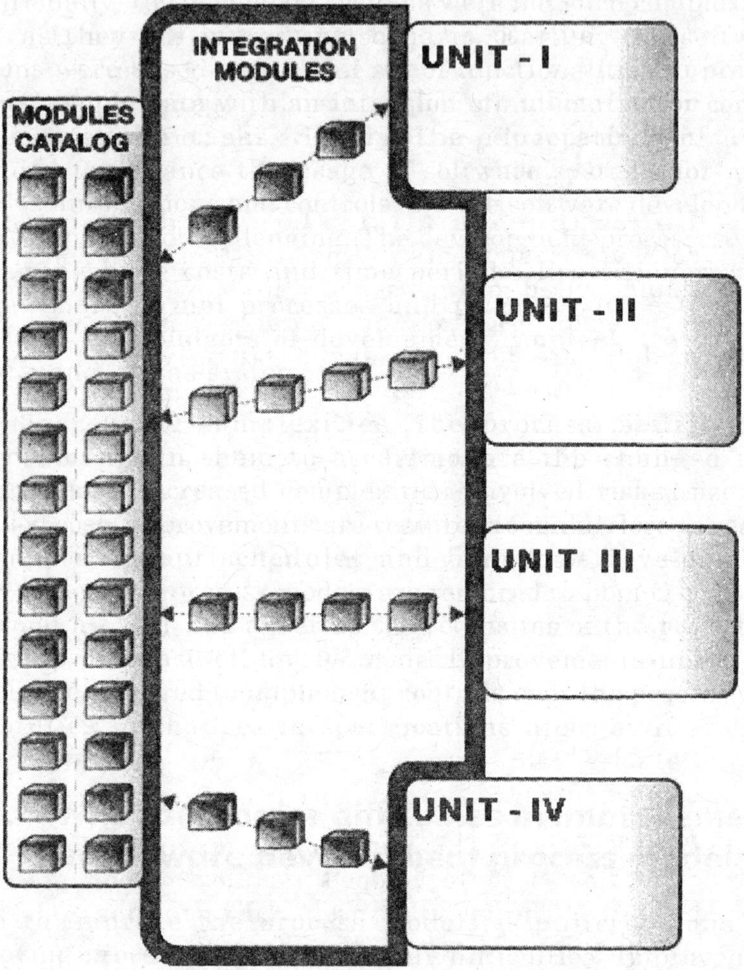

Figure 4.11: Module Integration into complete software system

- **Integration:** In the integration phase, the validated modules of the software are amalgamated by developing required interfaces as described in the design document. Maintaining consistency of the system during interfacing is of prime focus. Major activities in this phase are studying the communicating interfaces of each module as per the software design document, programming to implement these interfaces in the system and merging the modules with these interfaces to acquire the complete software system. The work products of this phase are program codes of interfaces used in integration of the system, common or shared data structure of integrated modules and the compiled integrated software.

- **System Testing:** System testing establishes confidence in the integrated system. The goal of system testing is to test the mutual effects of system components at run time and detecting presence of errors in the development. The unit testing phase determined accuracy and appropriateness of individual modules developed for the software. Now the goal is to validate the interfaces between them and the integrated system as a whole. System testing involves investigation and assessment of the complete system with other associated software or hardware components integrated together.

- **Installation & Operation:** This is the quiet obvious step after completion of development of the system. Here, in this step, the software is installed in the user's environment and its commands are handed over to customer. The users are provided with proper training, if and when required, to use the system. Although, the development phase is supposed to be over till this step but software development life cycle does not end here. This phase leads to another phase of testing where the consumer uses the software as per their requirements and expectation. This usage leads to discovery of hidden errors or faults left in the system during development. These errors are reported back to the developing team/ organization. Also the required changes and enhancements are notified to the team. Important work products are installation logs, operation logs, error reports and enhancement plans.

- **Maintenance:** Maintenance phase leads to corrections and enhancements in the functionality, quality and technology of the software. The error reported by the consumer while operation, are debugged in this phase.

The changes in the customer requirement during the course of the software usage are figured out and required enhancements in the software are made. Important activities in this phase are to make plans for debugging the errors left hidden in the software while its development, debugging and developing patches for the software to correct the new discovered errors, reanalyzing the complete software and enhancing its functionalities by adding new functional units in it, correcting the errors introduced during enhancement, technology up gradation and adaptation of the software to the new hardware or environment and improving its speed and quality by enhancing its design and structure. The important work products of this phase are enhanced test plans, software patches for correcting errors and enhancing functionalities, co-software for enhancement in technology or supporting new hardware and plans for new versions of the software.

Q. 7. Discuss Step-transition in Waterfall model.

Waterfall software development process model is a sequential pursue of development steps. Once a step is over, the process undergoes transition from that step to the other step. This transition is not random but governed by rules defined under the waterfall protocol. These rules can be summarized as follows:

1. **All steps occur sequentially without overlapping.** It is mandatory to carry out the steps of the waterfall model sequentially without any overlapping in them. No two steps can run in parallel. This is in agreement of sequential nature of the waterfall model.

2. **Engineers must complete one phase and close it formally before starting the next step** i.e. the new step can be entered only after the last step is concluded formally. For example, Designing can be started only after formal requirement specifications are completely defined and the coding & implementation can be done only after the design of the complete system and its components is formalized.

3. **While entering in a phase, results of the last step are taken as input or base for the new step.** This means, the requirement specifications defined in the requirement analysis phase becomes the basis of architecture of the system and its components.

4. **Once a step is closed, it cannot be reopened.** It is same as the journey of components of a waterfall on the cliff of a mountain. Once the water has flowed over the edge of the cliff and begun to fall down, it cannot turn back. Once the phase of development process is formally completed, the process proceeds to the next step with no turning back in waterfall model.

5. **No skipping of steps is allowed.** All the phases of the development through waterfall process model proceed in strict order with no step skipped. This may be observed quiet obvious because the next phase is based upon the results of the former. Hence, none of the steps may be skipped for proper base of the next step proceedings.

Q. 8. Discuss advantages of waterfall model of SDLC.

Waterfall model was derived from engineering practices to put some ordered sequence in phases of software development process for large projects. It consists of different stages of development that follow a strict linear order of execution to produce the complete software in one time. The model was found successful for many projects of history for its peerless advantages. Some of these advantages may be listed as follows:

1. **The model is simple and easy to understand.** This is because of its sequential nature that provides a well defined ordered procedure of software development and engineering activities. The model is also easily acceptable because of its simplicity and natural and obvious structure. Being like this, it is easy to be followed by engineers in practical environment.

2. **Easy to manage the project in this model.** This is because the steps of development follow a defined

sequence and are not executed in parallel. Only one phase of development run at a time. Hence the complete focus of developing team remains common and the resources are planed and controlled accordingly.

3. **Not much confusing because each step works on the results of the previous step.** Execution of each step is based upon results of the previous step. These results are the outcomes of extensive reworks and formal closure of the previous step and cannot be altered. Hence, the next step receives formal guide lines to work upon which makes its execution comparatively easy.

4. **Least space left for miscommunication between each development phase.** The next step receives a formal set of guidelines for its execution that leave the least space of miscommunications while carrying out the development steps. Also, non-parallel implementation of development phases reduces confusions between development phases.

5. **Waterfall model avoids the costs of iterations.** As this model executed the software development process in a sequential and non iterative manner, it forces to take utmost care to complete any phase of development before it is formally closed, because it is known that the closed step cannot be reopened (or the cost of reopening is too expensive). It avoids the needs of unwanted iterations and saves the consumption of excess resources and time.

6. **Easy to predict resources and time consumptions.** Waterfall model, as runs in a sequential manner and no iterations are entertained in the development life cycle, it is easy to predict resource consumption and time requirement for the each development phase and the total costs of development.

Although, these listed advantages demonstrate waterfall model as a strong choice for software development projects. But this model is not the ideal for all types of software development problems. It is stated that no model is found ideal for all problems and Waterfall model also suffers many inbuilt limitations in it. Some of these limitations are listed here.

Q. 9. What are major disadvantages of waterfall model of SDLC

Disadvantages/Limitations:

1. **Waterfall model is too restrictive to make iterations therefore is inflexible.** Practical projects rarely follow a sequential flow of development. Business and product requirements often change as the development proceeds, making a straight path to an end product unrealistic. Waterfall model states that once a step is formally declared closed, it cannot be reopened. If some faults are left in some step, which are caught later in the development cycle, reopening of that step in waterfall model and removal of those faults may be too expensive and even impractical in most of the cases.
2. **Not enough considerations of testing areas.** Waterfall model introduces testing steps in late phases of development life cycle. Testing in waterfall model is carried out only after complete implementation of software components. Due to testing late in development phases, the errors of implementation may be treated as removable but faults of design or mistakes in specifications are generally impractical to eliminate.
3. **Big experiences are needed to make a proper closure to perfect ness of each step.** Because, reopening a closed step in waterfall model is impractical, utmost care and extensive experience is required to declare a step ***complete & closed***. The results of each step must be extensively reanalyzed to be assured about their correctness and usability.
4. **Waterfall model supports very less interaction and involvement of the consumer of the product.** Waterfall model runs in a sequential non-iterative manner in which customer is involved and consulted during system analysis and requirement elicitation

phases. Once these specifications are freeze, they have no acquiescence to alter. After requirement elicitation phase is over, the consumer has almost no interaction with the developers. Due to this, most of the times, customer does have no idea of progress of the development he is waiting for. Also, the advantages of his feedback have to be compromised with.

5. **Waterfall model can be used only for well defined rigid requirement specifications.** As has been discussed, waterfall model does not allow any alteration in the specifications, once has been freeze. There is no provision to refine or redefine any part of the specifications in the due course of development. Hence, this model can be used only for a well defined and rigid problem statement and specification set which are not required to be re-cultured during development cycle.

6. **This model is not capable to respond to changes in expectations of the customer during development.** This is because of incapability of waterfall model to accommodate changes in the specifications in between the development cycle. The model gives the complete system all at once in the end of the development cycle where it is impractical to make changes in the software as per to accommodate changed expectations of the consumer and respective alterations in the specifications of the software.

7. **The procedure leads to a delayed exposure of serious errors or faults in specifications because working system is not available for test.** Waterfall model gives the complete software at one time only in the later phases of development. Due to this, the complete software is not available for testing. Due to delayed delivery of the software, the testing can be started in the later phases only. Due to this, serious errors left in the development are exposed very late where they are too expensive to be removed.

Q. 10. Explain Inflexibilities involved in the waterfall model and its disadvantages in software development.

Waterfall model of software development process is an inflexible model in terms of consent to change the specifications of the system or alteration in the results of development phases. The transitions among the steps of development are governed by firm rules. Any step, once closed formally, cannot be reopened in the course of development. Only one step can be executed at a time and no parallel execution of steps is followed. No step can be skipped and no alteration in sequence of steps is allowed. All these rules make the model an inflexible development process. These inflexibilities of the models where introduce some hindrances for the developers, in some other cases, these offer positively to improve the results.

Business and product requirements often change as the development proceeds, making a straight path to an end product realistic. On the negative sides, the inflexible nature of the waterfall model leads to incapability to accommodate changed requirements and expectations and alterations in design for better maintainability of the system. This inflexibility of the model results to deprived testing, late exposure to serious errors, late feeling of the real working system, very limited consumer involvement in the development cycle and need of long experience in similar projects etc.

Q. 11. Explain if the inflexibilities of waterfall model contribute positively to the development process or/and the product.

In spite of so many disadvantages of inflexible nature of waterfall model, the model serves to developer in many positive means too. These positive upshots are discussed here.

Positive upshots

1. **Visible state of progress:** Being inflexible non-iterative process, waterfall model is easily explainable for

it progress. The current development phase can clearly be explained because of no parallel execution of steps. The development team can clearly define the progress of development and state the current phase which the development is running in.

2. **Better project estimation and management:** Being sequential and start with rigid unalterable specifications, developer may better estimate the size, duration, difficulty, man power & resource consumption and other attributes of the project. There is almost no threat to add resource for iterations or alterations in design or specifications.

3. **High quality structural design:** Being started with rigid and unalterable specifications and experience of similar project problems, developers can produce a good and maintainable design right in the beginning of the project that can offer a quality base for development. Generally, outcomes of waterfall model are well structured and better maintainable and upheld for long existences.

4. **Robust base for each development phase:** Each step in the waterfall model is executed on the basis of the results of the previous steps. These results are published with utmost care and precautions with deliberation that no results can be altered in later phases. This leads to creation of a robust base for execution of steps.

5. **Least space for miscommunication between the steps:** Because, each step is executed based on robust results of the previous steps. These results are published in a very formal manner in the form of stiff documents viz. Software Requirement Specification Document (SRSD), Software Design Document (SDD), Unit Test Plan, System Test Plan, Maintenance Plan etc. These documents are created with apposite consistency, correctness and reliability. These formal documents overrule most of miscommunications and misconceptions between different phases of development.

Figure 4.12: Inflexibility gives rigidity & positive results

Q. 12. What is Evolutionary Software Development?

It has been found that business and consumer requirements change their shapes and viability during development of the software. It makes the sequential software development impractical. Developers first need to explore through the consumer requirements thoroughly and both, the consumer and the developer, need to come to a common specification set that will finally be translated into a detailed design and coded into the final implementation. Also it is tough to formally define a non-existing and unseen product. Further, the specifications are the basis of the contract between the customer and the developer. Business contracts cannot be agreed on abstract and ambiguous basis or will result to bad relations in future. Hence, it becomes a necessity to work on the formal and explicit specifications. For detailed understanding of the system, it is advisable to work with a working model of the complete system that gives a direct feeling of the system itself. These working models are called prototypes and are developed in consultations of the consumer and required alterations in the functionality of the system are quickly implemented. This approach of software development with active involvement of the consumer is called evolutionary approach.

In the evolutionary approach, the software is the result of multiple iterations and modifications in order to meet consumer requirements. The process starts with an abstract and incomplete specification set. This incomplete specification set is quickly designed and implemented into a working model called prototype. The primary focus of development of a prototype is to understand the functional behavior of the expected system and not the performance attribute. The functional model of the system is consulted with the consumer and feedback is captured. The requirement specifications of the system are then refined as per the feedback. New functionalities are added and design constraints are discussed. The model is then refined as per the new specifications and the process of refinement of specifications and prototype is iterated till inclusion of all functional and performance expectations of the consumer.

Q. 13. What are key advantages of Evolutionary Software Development?

Evolutionary software development addresses many limitations of sequential development. Advantages of evolutionary development model are discussed here.

1. **Active consumer involvement:** Evolutionary model allows active participation of the consumer in software development life cycle. Here the consumer gives its feedback about the system from time to time and accordingly, the specifications and designs are altered. Results of each of the iterations are sent to the consumer for feedback and iterations continue till mutual acceptance of the system by consumer and developer.

2. **Ability to accommodate changes and refinement in specifications and designs:** Unlike sequential development models, evolutionary model allows moderate changes and refinement in the system specifications in early phase of development. A working model or prototype of the existing system is provided to the user

and feedback is captured and changes in specifications and designs are made to meet user's expectations.

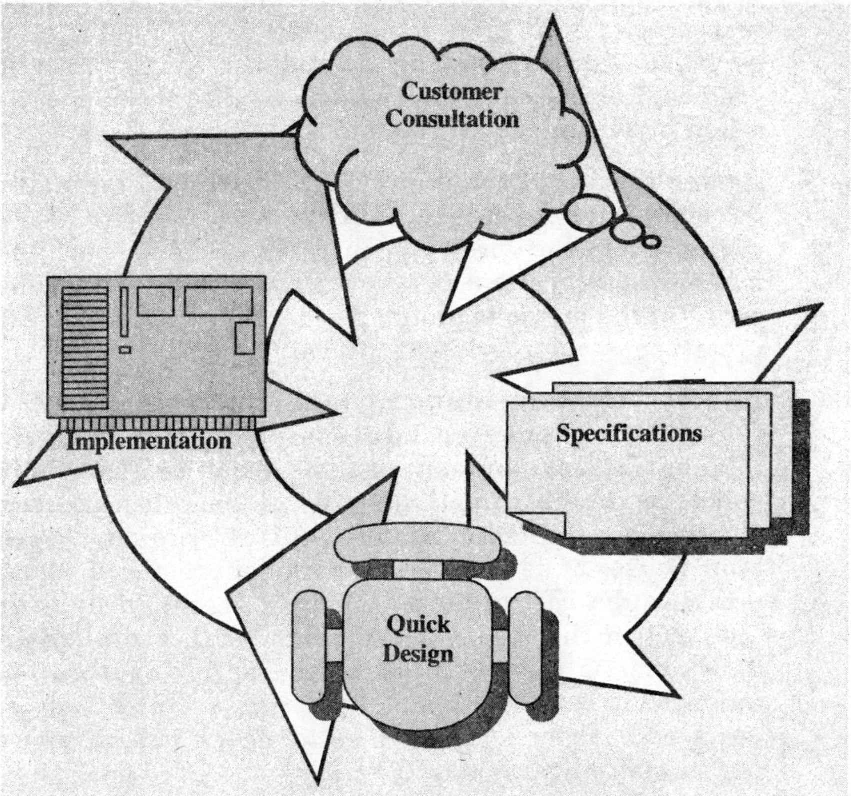

Figure 4.13: Evolutionary Development Model.

3. **Quick feel of real system, hence better understanding of it:** Quick implementation of specifications into a prototype gives an early feel of the final product. It helps in better understanding the system. It makes in depth analysis of the final system possible with its working prototype before the actual system completes. It helps in better modifications and up gradation in designs. Types of required maintenance of the system and technology up gradations can be better predicted and accommodated in evolutionary development process.

4. **Early exposure of serious faults/errors of the system:** Evolutionary model provides a quick and in depth analysis of the real system with a working prototype of it. It gives a better feel of the final system by which; serious future errors and discrepancies can be predicted quiet early and remedy modifications can be taken in design of the system.

5. **Better testing:** Each prototype is tested and evaluated on consumer's scales. Testing and modifications evaluation of each prototype discover errors in them and modifications are done to remove those errors. Hence, the errors of the previous prototypes are removed in the next prototype by appropriate modifications.

6. **Phase wise development makes possible better feasibility checks so addressing to risk factors:** Sequential development models produce the whole software in one run. Hence all the modules and sub modules are treated of.equal risk. If the project fails in later phases of development for the failure of some high risk module, cost of development of all the modules is included in the loss. On the other hand, evolutionary development models allow software development in multiple iterations. Hence, high risk modules may be developed earlier in order to better check risk of failure and minimize losses.

7. **Options for better budgeting& utilization of resources:** Phase wise development in evolutionary models can provide a better budgeting of the system. Most of time, business units have a flow of money and resources. Also, companies may be working on multiple projects and teams of some special expertise may be working on some other projects. In the evolutionary model, instead of hiring additional resources for the current project, the work may be distributed among the team of experts and some of the modules may be worked earlier whereas some other may be developed later, when the required resources let free. This allows a better utilization of existing resources.

Q. 14. Discuss major disadvantages of Evolutionary SDLC models.

Following are the disadvantages of an evolutionary software development process model:

1. **The process is not visible.** The process of development starts with incomplete or ambiguous specifications set that is refined in consultation with the consumer. Refinement of specifications is an indeterminate process, the end of which can not be determined, because one cannot determine how much time it will take to meet consumers' needs. Also, as the process goes on, consumer keeps changing it expectations. Evolutionary model is enabled for accommodating these changes but it consumes time to make changes and the project progress is delayed and conducted to an invisible process.

2. **Software systems are usually poorly structured.** This is because the evolutionary software is an outcome of multiple alterations and chain of modifications in the purpose, functionality and design of the software. During refinement in the specifications and respective modifications in the software are generally implemented quickly without making appropriate revision in the design and structure of the system. Due to this, the resultant software is not well structured and maintainable.

3. **Special skills are required to control the process, or the process may lead to an endless practice.** As discussed, generally, Business and product requirements often change as the development proceeds. Consumer expands its expectations during the course of development. It is quiet natural for any human, because as the user becomes a part of system development, it starts understanding the system in depth and extends its expectations from the system. Due to this, more and more modifications are made in the software. A sophisticated & clever and skilled management is desired

to control the project and prevent it from becoming an endless and uncontrollable process.

4. **Strong planning is required or the process may overshoot in resource and time consumption.** Consumer is directly an actively involved throughout the process of evolutionary software development. It allows the consumer to directly interact with the developers and direct them as per its expectations. Customers have tendency to change requirements from the software under development. It leads to unexpectedly large number of iterations while prototyping and refining specifications. Quiet strong planning and coordination is required to control iterations to reach to the final specification set as per user requirements.

5. **Good business analysts are required throughout the process or it may become a victim of consumer frustration.** Business analyst is responsible for translating informal requirements and expectations of technology-ignorant customer into technology-adaptive formal specifications. Continuously changing consumer requirements may create inconsistencies in development and business analyst is expected to remove them smartly. Further, the business analyst should also control the changes in expectations smartly without hurting business relations with customer.

Q. 15. Discuss or compare the usefulness of Waterfall model vs. that of Evolutionary SDLC Models

Waterfall model where follows a sequential flow to give a well structured maintainable product, there evolutionary models are capable of accommodating the alterations in designs and specifications of the product. Both the models are preferred for different types of cases and different types of problems in hand. The usefulness of each model is compared here.

1. **Type of project:** Choice of an appropriate process model for development mainly depends on the type of the

project in hand. Waterfall model is expected to be a good choice in the projects with rigid and well defined specifications. On the other hand, evolutionary model is the choice of the projects with incomplete or ambiguous specifications. Evolutionary project development provides a fair consumer interaction for refinement of specifications and better understanding of the system, whereas waterfall model provides strong project planning with close estimations of their size, cost and duration.

2. **Type of experience:** Waterfall model is expected to give good results with a team having good experience in similar types of problems and technology. On the other hand, evolutionary model is a better choice for a new and unknown problem or unknown environment. This is because, on the basis of their experience, the development team can predict the types of risks, technology constraints, environmental consequences and design-requirements for a given problem. But for a newer problem, they may need exposure and exploration to better understand the problem and propose a solution. They may also be required to check the reliability and consistency of their proposed solution. The solutions may be required to modify to rule out caught errors. Hence, for an unseen problem or environment, evolutionary model is found to be more useful. But, for a worked out problem, waterfall model can give faster and cheaper results.

3. **Type of consumer & requirements:** The project where the consumer is expected to change their requirements very frequently, evolutionary model may be a better choice than the waterfall model. Waterfall model will not be able to accommodate changes in consumer requirements during the course of development. Also in the cases where the customer is not quiet clear or intelligent about its requirements or where it may not define the requirements clearly, waterfall model results to failure. On the other side, in the projects with well defined specifications, or the type of projects where

requirements have already been implemented and reengineering of the product is required, waterfall model is an obvious choice.

4. **Type of system complexity:** Complex systems are required to be developed with more care and in depth understanding of the system. These systems need an excellent design to enhance its life and enhancibility. Evolutionary models provide detailed analysis of the system but they provide a poor structure of the system. On the other hand, waterfall model provide a good structure of the design of the system but it does not provide opportunity of better understanding of the system.

5. **Type of progress visibility:** If the project is on a critical schedule and resource management plan, the development process model is required to have a visible progress measurement. The project in waterfall model is better controllable in terms of time schedules and resource consumption. On the other hand, evolutionary models generally suffer from time and cost overshoots because of uncontrolled and elongated consumer involvement.

Q. 16. Discuss different Threats involved in evolutionary models.

Evolutionary software development is about engineering software with active and continuous participation of the consumer in the development process. Although, this is a good approach for better understanding and implementation of consumer expectations and achieving better customer satisfaction. Yet, the approach suffers many threats of project failure inbuilt in it. Some selective of these threats are discussed here.

1. **Development may fall into an endless process.** Evolutionary models are directed with active involvement of the consumer in the development process and consumer have tendency of varying requirement specifications of the software. Consumer generally gets

divert from its high preference requirements. It leads to continual iterations in the development life cycle.

2. **Cost of development may overshoot the budget.** Business and product requirements often change as the development proceeds. Accommodating these alterations in the specifications consume extra resources and time. In spite of exercising based on the best project planning practices, number of iterations increase beyond expectations. It elongates the process and the cost overshooting is quite obvious in such cases.

3. **Projects may get delayed beyond expectation.** Unexpected changes in specifications and accommodation of alterations in specifications increase the number of iterations and refinement cycles in the development. It generally elongates the development cycle and delay the release of the final software.

4. **Project may face loss in consumer interest.** Sometimes, when the development process overruns in time due to unanticipated and astonishing alterations in business requirements and the system specifications, consumer loses its interest in the system development. It may be because of many reasons viz. consumer may have started with some other tasks of more importance for it or the consumer may feel the process more strenuous as it was ever expected. In such a case, it becomes almost impossible to keep the project live.

5. **A good contract and mutual understanding is required from both (developer and customer) side, or the project face unwanted complexities in their business relations.** Due to lost or degraded customer interest in the project or due to many other reasons, the customer may not be showing proper attention towards the project. On the other side, the company may have substantial planning and expectations from the project. This may lead to impairment of business relations between the two parties. Hence a strict contract with mutual understanding is required for the success of the project.

Q. 17. What is Prototyping SDLC model?

Prototyping model emphasizes on development of a working model of the real system and evolving it with consultation with the consumers as per their requirements and expectations. This process allows the developers to understand consumer expectations in a better way. Thus, the prime focus of development of the prototype is to understand the functional behavior of the system and customer prospect. The prototype is evolved and refined in multiple iterations according to the feedbacks of users for its functionalities, outlook and performance. These iterations are continued till consumer satisfies with the functionalities and performance of the system. Finally the required system s delivered to the customer.

Q. 18. What are different types of prototype models popular in industrial practices? Explain each in short notes.

There are basically two types of prototyping model:

1. **Exploratory Development model:** This model lay on quick development of a prototype based on the initial specifications narrated by the customer. The prototype is evaluated by consumer and required alterations in the functionality of the system are reported. The prototype is refined and tested as per the requirements and given to the consumer for reevaluation. The process is continued till consumer satisfies. In the exploratory prototyping model, the final prototype that meets all consumer expectations and is mutually accepted by the developer and customer is delivered to the consumer after a few revisions and modifications. It means that, in exploratory prototype model, the prototype itself is converted into the final product through a number of explorations and evolutions and delivered to the customer.

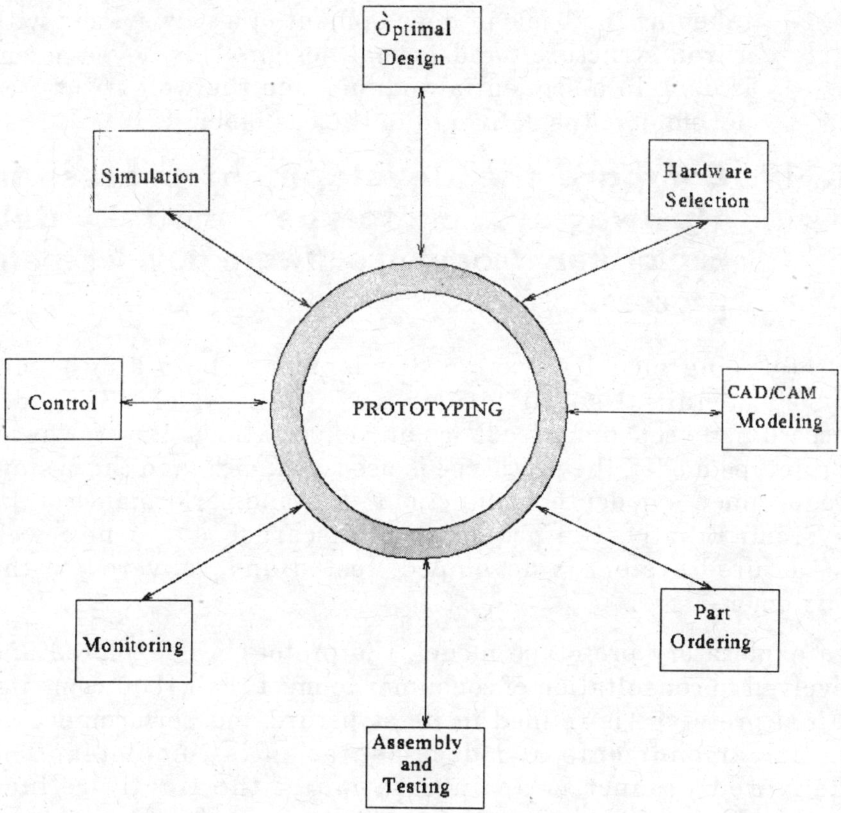

Figure 4.14: Different ways of prototyping

2. **Throwaway Prototyping Model:** This model also starts with initial prototype that is evolved with consumer consultation. In this model, the objective of evolution of prototype is merely to understand the functional requirement and working of the system and accordingly update the system requirement specifications. Finally, the specifications are prepared as per the final prototype that meet consumer requirements and is mutually accepted by the developers and the customer. But in throwaway prototype software development model, the prototype is not for delivery to the customer. The finally refined specifications are now

taken as the basis of development of a new system with a well structured and formal design. This development is done in a sequential manner and the well structured development is delivered to the customer.

Q. 19. Compare the development process in Throwaway prototype model and Exploratory Model of software development process.

Prototyping model works on development of working model based on initial specifications and evolution of this model according to consumer feedback and expectations. In throwaway prototype model, the prototype is used to understand the system requirements in depth for functionalities and performance of the system. Finally, the prototype is discarded and a new well structured system is developed, tested and delivered to the customer.

In exploratory prototype model, the prototype is explored and evolved in consultation of consumer to meet their requirements. Final prototype is refined in its structure and performance by minor amendments and documentation is completed. The delivered product is an integration of the finally refined prototype and its documentation.

The comparison between the two processes can be summarized as follows:

Both the processes start with initial, incomplete specifications of the system as narrated by the customer and a working prototype is implemented for evaluation by consumer. In throwaway prototype, the implementation is done quickly in order to represent the functionality of the system and none other attribute of its quality whereas, in exploratory prototyping, because same prototype after refinement is to be delivered, quality is equally important right from initial prototypes. Hence, an equal attention is given towards the structure and performance of the system. Further, whenever the prototype is refined, throwaway prototype process concentrates on functionality implementation only whereas; exploratory process focuses on its quality also. Ultimately, when a prototype meets all requirements of consumer and mutually accepted by the developer and the customer, it is named as final prototype. For the exploratory development, the same prototype is refined into the final product and documentation is integrated in it. On the other hand, in throwaway prototype model, this prototype is used to generate a refined set of specifications that meet all expectations of the consumer or user of the system. These specifications are then translated into a high quality design and implemented. The final implementation is tested and delivered for usage. Hence, the two processes differ in their end products and their qualities also.

Q. 20. Discuss advantages of throwaway prototype over exploratory prototype delivery.

Throwaway prototyping and exploratory prototype, both are commonly used evolutionary development processes in software development. Exploratory model where focuses towards development of a well structured prototype meeting the abstract requirement set and exploring it up till it meets user expectations, throwaway prototype on the other hand, meets to understand user needs with the help of a quickly designed prototype and after proper understanding of these requirements, a formal requirement specifications set is created. The prototype is discarded and the system is developed from scratch based on the refined formal specification.

The following are the merits of throwaway prototype over exploratory prototype delivery:

1. Throwaway prototype development may start with the least understood and most abstract specifications whereas inception of exploratory prototype begins with a more formal specification that will expect fewer changes in it.

2. Throwaway prototype is developed very quickly and is produced for evaluation of functional expectations and hence provides a quick impression of the actual system. It allows use of informal shortcuts in development whereas exploratory prototype is a more formal

development that follows all formalities of the process and standards of the process. It may be proved to be a slow and uneasy practice to apply formal methods and standards working with abstract specifications.

3. Throwaway prototype provides a meaning to understand the user expectations in depth and finally it is discarded and a new and formal system is developed under well-defined standards of quality. This practice allows producing high quality product that is well structured, user-friendly and highly maintainable. On the other hand, exploratory development is about exploring the prototype and developing it into the final product by adding up to accommodate the newly understood requirements in the prototype and finally refining the system. This practice most of the times, proves to produce unstructured and unmentionable products. Exploratory software generally contains less cohesive and highly coupled modules that are tough to test and alter.

4. Throwaway prototyping methodology usually produces more efficient, testable and maintainable products as compared to exploratory practices. This is because of redesigning and re-implementation of the complete system after understanding the expectations and requirements.

Q. 21. What are the disadvantages/limitations of throwaway prototype over exploratory prototype delivery?

Following are the demerits of throwaway prototype over exploratory prototype delivery:

1. For a very large and complex system, making and controlling a throwaway prototype in a rough and quick manner may be too expensive and impractical. Instead, an exploratory prototype may be a better choice for it's more formal, maintainable and controllable structure.

2. Throwaway prototype, as compared to the exploratory prototype sometimes fails especially in the projects where

some quality attributes of the system such as performance, throughput, and response time of the system are required to be demonstrated in the prototype itself. It happens usually with development of the machines that work in reference of the real time clocks.

3. Throwaway prototyping practices give an illusion of wasting resources as after preparing a formal and complete specification document, the prototype is discarded and a newest system is developed under formal practices. The exploratory development on the other side uses the outcomes of all the efforts made during exploration and adding onto the past prototypes evolves the system.

4. Throwaway prototype sometimes leads a risk of consumer displeasure when after demonstrating the expected system, the developing team asks for some more time to develop a new system. It may be hard for customer to understand the need of developing another new system meeting his requirements instead of delivering the prototype itself.

Q. 22. Explain Spiral evolutionary software process model.

Barry Boehm defined the spiral model of software development in his article **"A Spiral Model of Software Development and Enhancement"** in 1985. Spiral model of software development can accommodate most of the early models as its special cases and also provides advantages of hybrid models that are the combination of tow or more different models created as and when required. This model of development combines the features of the prototyping model, the waterfall model and other early practicing models. The spiral model is favored for large, expensive, and complicated projects. Spiral model provides a significant management control over the process by demonstration of some data of that importance. The radial dimension of the spiral progress-graph of the project demonstrated the cumulative cost incurred in the project till date. The angular dimension of the progress graph here demonstrates the progress made in each iteration cycle. Each spiral cycle begins with the identification of the objectives of the cycle, its work product, different alternatives available for implementation of work product and the constraints involved with each implementation alternative. Each alternative along with its constraints is accessed and reviewed for its areas of uncertainties and risks. Formal strategies are planned and carried out after the review of the each alternative and their involved risks and the developments are implemented. The work products are provided to the customer for evaluation and comments along with the required alterations are documented. The next cycle is then planned for its objectives and strategies and the process continues.

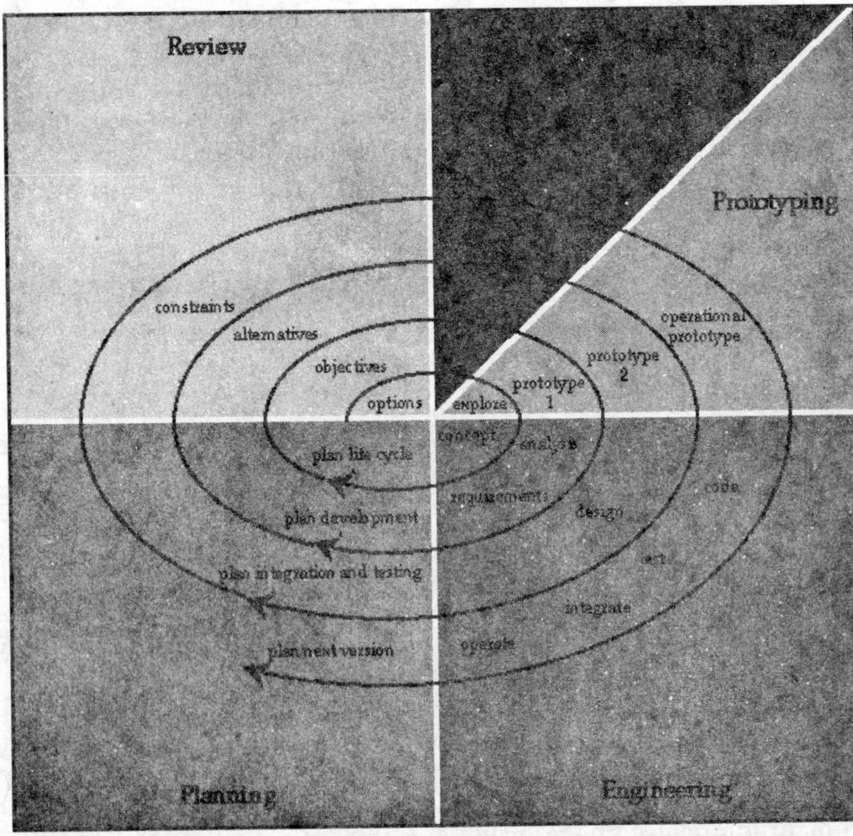

Figure 4.15: Spiral Model of Software Development

Q. 23. Explain different phases in Spiral SDLC and discuss activities executed in each of them in brief.

There are basically four phases in spiral model: Planning, Review, Risk Analysis and Engineering. These four phases are iteratively in multiple cycles followed one after other. These phases in the model may be briefly described as follows:

- **Planning Phase:** Planning phase is about to plan the work products, strategies and resources of the cycle. In this phase, the objectives, alternatives and constraints of the project are planned and officially documented. The specifications of the product and process of the cycle are drafted and different available alternatives for implementation are presented formally.
- **Risk Analysis Phase:** On of the most important and exclusive feature of Spiral model is the risk analysis phase involved in it. In this phase all available alternatives of implementing the development in a cost effective manner are analyzed and reviewed. This phase has been added specially in order to identify, discuss and resolve the possible risks in the project early in the development cycle. If risk is associated due to uncertainties of requirement specifications, prototyping may be taken as an option to reduce its effect.
- **Engineering Phase:** After risk analysis, the actual implementation of the project is carried out and the work products are developed in accordance of the strategies drafted in the previous steps of the cycle. The work products of this phase may either be another prototype or module or subsystem or the system itself.
- **Customer Evaluation Phase:** In this phase, the engineering work products are presented for customer evaluation to receive review comments and suggestions to alter that may help in identifying and resolving potential problems and bugs in the developed.

Q. 24. What are the merits of spiral process model over the other evolutionary process models?

Spiral model is a type of evolutionary software development models that works for software development with continual participation of the consumer and refinements in specifications as per expectations of the customer. After a significant number of iterations, and a number of prototype evaluations, the final product is released, installed, operated and maintained. In conjunction with other features of evolutionary models, spiral model is involves a formal risk analysis in each iteration of development cycle. Spiral model shows not only the steps of development life cycle but also shows some planning or management aspects in its portrayal structure viz. radius of the spiral curve shows cumulative resource consumption it development to achieve some point on the development curl and the angular movement shows the process progress in the current iteration. The number of cycles in the spiral curve shows the number of iterations passed in the development process. Spiral software development is mainly a risk conscious software development model and in this manner it proves to be stronger approach than traditional software development process models. Spiral model provides a formal risk analysis and risk report that ay be assessed for any feedback in case of crisis. Spiral model couples the iterative nature of prototyping models with controlled and systematic aspects of sequential model along with mathematical control over the process.

Q. 25. What are major limitations & disadvantages of Spiral model in practice?

Although, spiral model contains all advantages of traditional process models along with extra features of benefits, yet, like other process models, even this model could not be proved to be ideal for all types of problems. The model has some limitations and inbuilt disadvantages with it.

The spiral model of software development process provides excess of flexibility in the process and may be difficult to convince that the evolutionary process is controllable. Further, the risk assessment process bears a significant cost and time consumption. Hence, spiral model with such resource consumption can not be considered as a good choice for the problems of low risks and less development complexities.

Also the risk assessment exercise demands extensive expertise and the results of the practice rely on the expertise of the practitioners. As the model processes relied on the risk assessment reports, the incompleteness or incorrectness of the risk analysis may lead to a major loss of development by occurrence of an undiscovered risk in the process.

The spiral software development model uses prototyping as a risk reduction mechanism but, more important, enables the developers to apply prototyping approach at any stage of evolution of the product. It maintains the classic stepwise approach for software development but incorporates it into an iterative framework that more realistically reflects the real world. Spiral model demands a direct and formal consideration of technical risks at all stages of software development project and, if properly applied, should reduce risks before they become problematic and knotty.

Q. 26. Explain Iterative enhancement software process model.

In the iterative incremental enhancement, the software is developed in an incremental manner that allows the developer to take advantage of its experiences during the development of earlier, incremental, deliverable versions of the system. The project is completed in multiple iterations and the products are released in multiple versions. Each of the multiple iterations is made through inception, elaboration, implementation and transition phases. The Procedure itself consists of the Initialization and Iteration steps, and the Project Control List. The initialization step focuses on a base version of the system. The goal for this initial implementation is to create a product to which the user can react. Most of the high priority requirements or the requirements of high risks are implemented in the base version that offers a sampling of the key aspects of the problem and provide a solution that is simple manner. To guide the iteration process, a project control list and version plans are created. The version plan tracks the changed and functional or nonfunctional enhancements to be made in the consecutive versions of the product. The most well known iterative development frameworks are the Rational Unified Process and the Dynamic Systems Development Method.

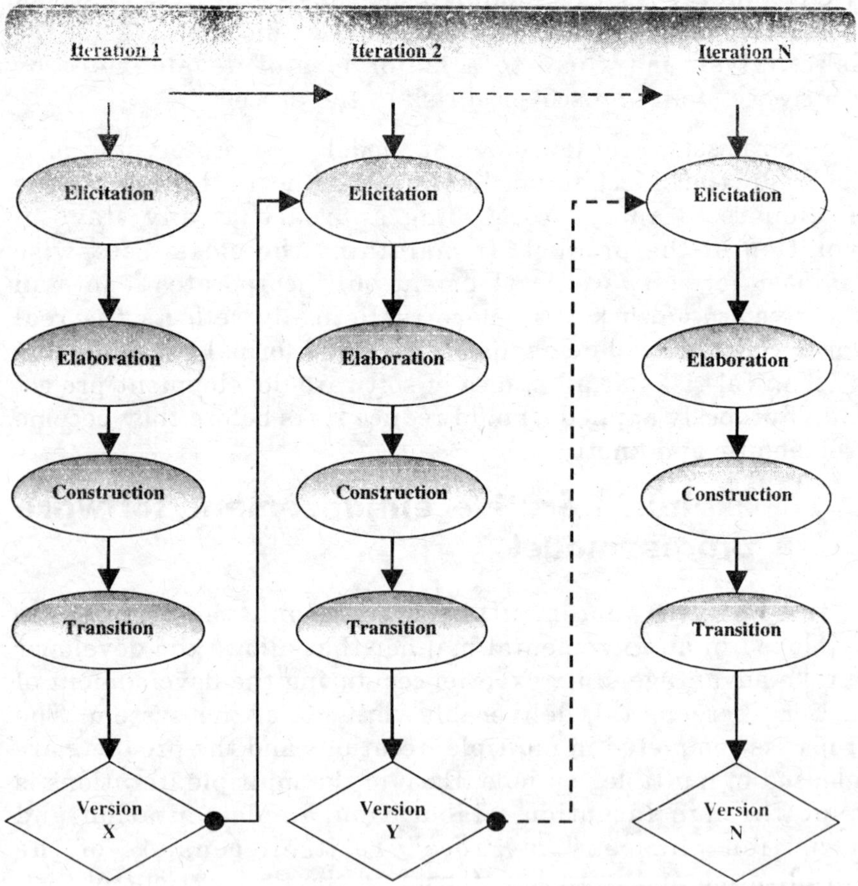

Figure 4.16: Iterative Enhancement Model

Q. 27. What is the difference between Iterative enhancement software process model and prototyping models?

Incremental enhancement model is quite different from prototyping and must not be misunderstood in the same manner. In prototyping, focus of developers was to first understand the user requirements & evolve the software in an exploratory manner. In prototyping, the developer as well as the customer keeps learning the fact about the system and keep enhancing their requirements. It gives major changes in the basic SRS of the project. On the other hand, in the iterative enhancement process, much of the formal specifications are prepared in the beginning of the process and later only some minor changes are made as per needs. The basic focus of iterative enhancement process is not merely to enhance the SRS but the focus is to implement the high priority and high risk features early so that the loss on probable failure of the project may be minimized. Also, releasing software in multiple version allows to control the huge projects and work on them phase wise so that the complete big project may be divided into smaller work-products that may be produced one after the other by enhancing the early products of the process.

Q. 28. Discuss the advantages of releasing any software in multiple phases rather than in a single go.

There are many obvious advantages of releasing the software in multiple versions. While developing another enhanced version of software, the design of the previous version may be taken as a base and only the minimum required changes are made in the system in order to implement the enhancements in minimum efforts and cost. The multiple versions of the software allow better customization of the software. If enhancement of the system in a required manner is found very tough and costly, it may be opted with another previous version that may allow such major enhancements in a cheaper manner. Also, as the enhanced software will obviously be higher in cost for the consumer, the consumer can budget the project in a better way and ask to implement the high priority requirements first and later as the resources are arranged enough, the product may be enhanced. Different communities of user also get multiple options for functionalities and performance of the software and hence they are provided with multiple choices that they may decide as per their own satisfaction. As the requirement of the user may change with time, releasing the software in multiple iterations also save the cost of implementing the requirements of low priorities that may later be removed from the list for better alternatives. Version control over the project allows understanding the pros and cones of the decisions made during the process and the mistake may be corrected well in time before they become prominent and all most impossible to cover.

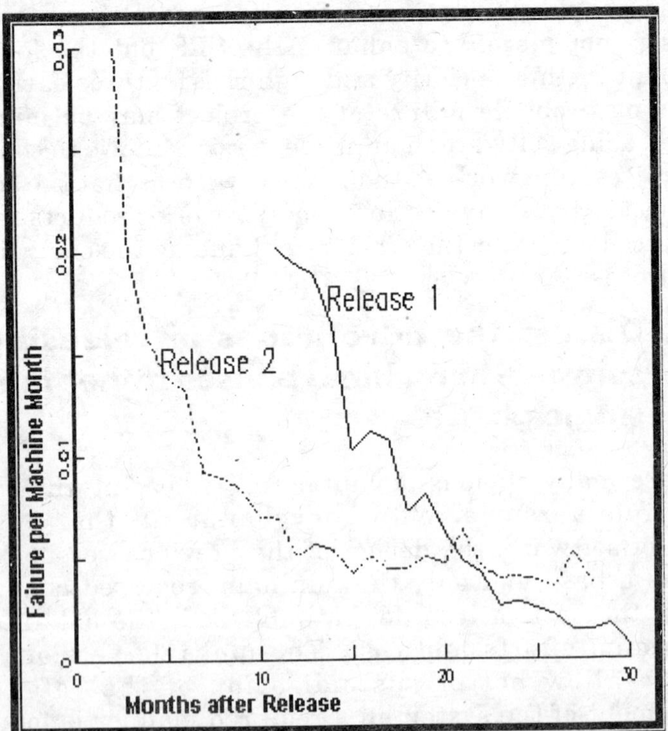

Figure 4.17: Reduction in Failure Rate in subsequent released versions of software

Q. 29. Explain differences between a prototype & software version.

A prototype is a quick and rough implementation of what is understood by initial and incomplete specifications and that may not be satisfying all of the expectations of the consumer in terms of its functional and non-functional requirements like throughput, response time, simplicity etc. A prototype is developed with a focus of requirement elaboration and understanding the system better. Another focus of prototyping may be to verify the feasibility of the ideas for minimizing the risk of failure due to lack of experience and exposures. On the other hand, version of software is released formally and is complete software that has officially been published by the developing company for its user(s). The early versions of the software may not be including all the planned functionalities yet it formally meets the partial requirements of the system with standard documents and quality attributes. While prototyping, the hidden or ambiguous aspects of the system are implemented first so that these areas may be explored for understanding them better. On the other hand, in a version plan, the high priority requirements along with the high risk specifications are implemented first. In the early versions of the software, the priority of implementation may be assigned to the functional and non functional requirements ma be assigned according to their importance for the user to work with the system, or according to the risk involved to implement them, or according to the degree of dependence of the project success on them or a combination of them. As per their priority of implementation, these specifications are planned for version wise implementation and a formal version plan is created that describes the number of versions planned for publishing of the complete software and the functional contents of each version. Each version is planned and completed individually and formally on the standards of process and product quality. The version is implemented with a plan of its enhancement to the next planned version(s). The same is not true for prototyping. The prototyping is done not with a plan of releasing the software in multiple versions but the complete software is produced in one run. The partial functionalities are quick developed for exploring the system with a real feel. Also, in prototyping, the priorities of implementation are not that strict as in version plans. The prototyping also does not require meeting quality standards for non functional requirements like response time, throughput, speed etc. Only the final system, prepared for formal release is required to meet the expected standards.

Q. 30. What is Capability Maturity Model (CMM)? Explain the Structure of CMM.

Capability Maturity Model (CMM) is not a process model for software development, but it is a model that describes the maturity of the organization or the team developing the software

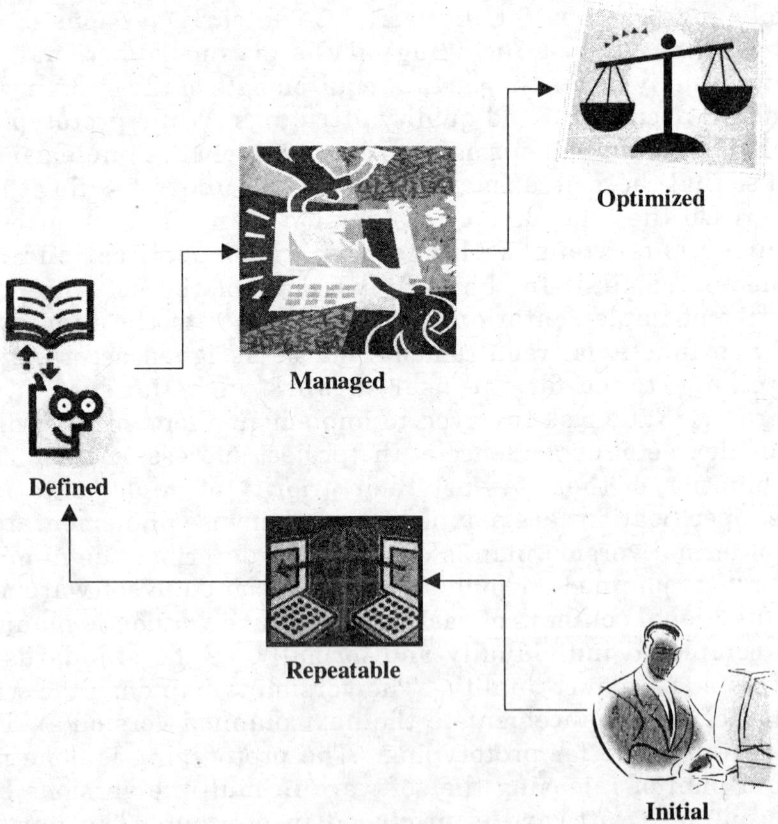

Figure 4.18: Levels in Capability Maturity Model

and the process of development. Capability Maturity Model was defined by Software Engineering Institute (SEI) of Carnegie Mellon University along with many other organizations with an intention of measuring the efficiency and sense of maturity of the process of development.

In its structure, CMM categorizes hierarchically, the software developing organizations on the basis of the maturity of their process, in five distinct levels. Each of these levels is defined with set of process goals associated with them. These levels are defined as follows:

1. **Initial:** The first and the lower most CMM level is named as "Initial". At this level, most of the processes run on ad-hoc practices and the success of the process depends on the expertise of developers. But the success histories do not repeat so often in any defined manner. This is due to unavailability or non-adoption of any formal method with retainable documentations. The process at "Initial" level is disorganized and crisis probable.

2. **Repeatable:** Second lowest level of CMM is named as "Repeatable". At this level, strategies for carrying out the development process are formally planned and development is tracked. As the name of the level suggests, the process is repeatable for its success because of its formal planning.

3. **Defined:** At the Third level from bottom of the hierarchy in CMM comes the "Defined" level where the process of development is formally defined at all levels of organization. A formal organizational constitution is defined that is followed at all levels of development to develop a formal management control over the process.

4. **Managed:** At the next level of CMM, organizations establish metrics and measured controls over the process. This leads to a fair management of the process with quantitative definitions of goals and process to achieve these goals.

5. **Optimization:** The top most level of CMM is "Optimization", where the goal of the organization is not

only the user satisfaction ad development of highly efficient software but also to contribute to their social and ethical responsibilities towards software practices in a formal manner. At this level, the organizations not only work for betterment of products but also of the process. This level in CMM has a set goal of making improvements in traditional processes of software development.

Q. 31. Discuss the importance of CMM in software industry.

Capability Maturity Model is important to compare the software engineering processes for maturity of their approach and efforts to improve the software products and development processes for better quality, and better process control. Capability Maturity Model is used as a guideline for software process improvement efforts. Capability Maturity Model categorize the different software development organizations on the basis of their contribution to the software market in terms of improvement in software product quality by enhancing development life cycle process. Is specifies the ethical and social responsibilities associated with the development procedures for software. CMM describes the parallel importance of process improvements along with product improvement as user satisfaction. CMM introduces hierarchy in software industry based on maturity of the works of some organization.

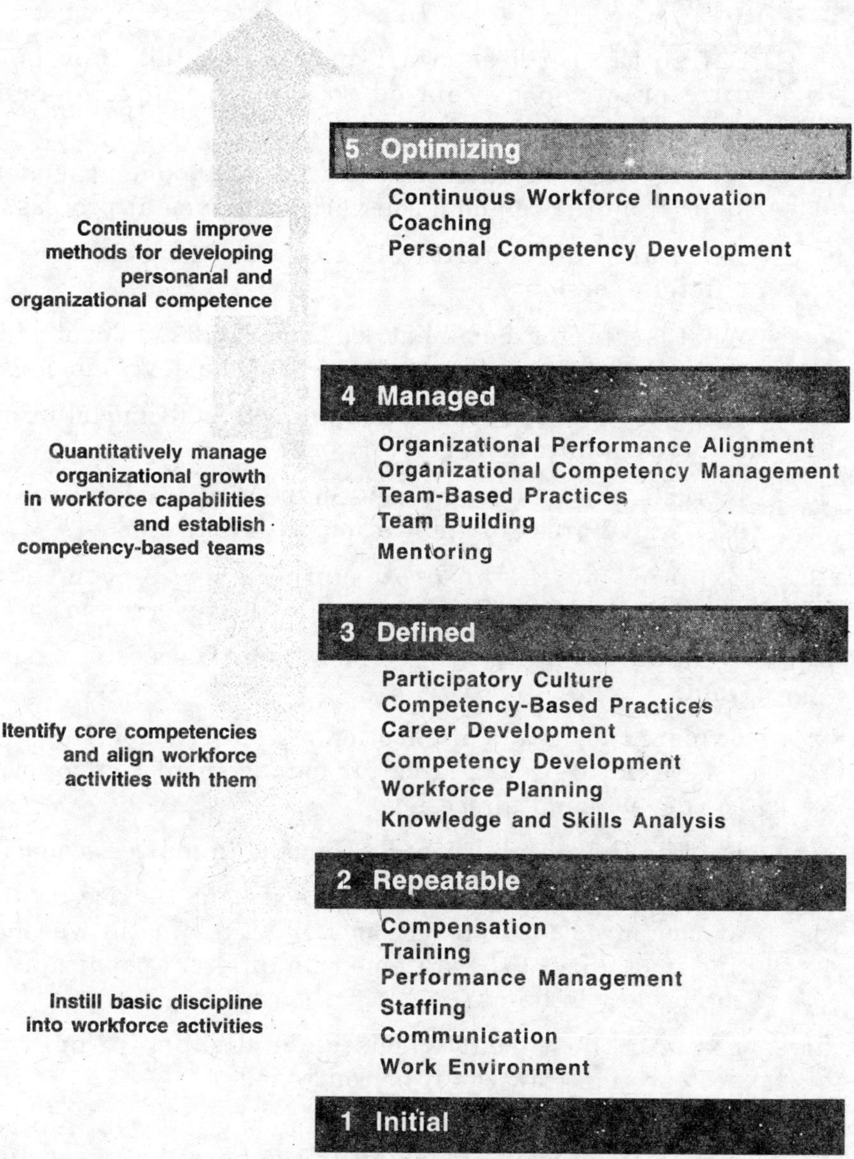

Figure 4.19: Application & responsibilities of CMM

Exercises

i. Define the term software process model. How is it different from or related to software development process?

ii. Why do we need different software development models apart from the common software development process?

iii. What are the benefits of releasing the software in different versions?

iv. What is a prototype? What are the benefits of developing prototype of any software before its true development?

v. What are different limitations of waterfall model? How can these limitations be overcome?

vi. Describe the limitations of V-Shape model. What are the best suited areas of application of V-Shape model?

vii. Explain merits of prototyping over incremental enhancement of software. Explain the reverse too.

viii. What do you mean by a version plan? Discuss a version plan.

ix. Explain the area of application of spiral model. How can it be used to provide a better management control over the development process?

x. Explain the suitability of RAD model in today's scenario.

xi. "Waterfall model give a much precise and concise results as compared to prototype model". Explain the validity and invalidity of the statement in different conditions of the project in hand.

xii. Explain the threat of customer disappointment in prototyping. How can it be controlled?

xiii. What should be a better choice among different process models for development of any general software like library information system or inventory management system? Explain your choice.

xiv. What is a better choice among process models to address tight schedules and cost of the software precisely?

References

1. Aggarwal, K.K., Singh, Y. (2001), *Software Engineering*, New Age Publishers, New Delhi
2. Bersoff, E.H. and Davis, A.M. (1991), *Impact of Lifecycle Models on Software Configuration Management*, Communication ACM, 34(8), 104-118.
3. Bhasker J. (1999), *VHDL Primer*, 3rd Edition, Prentice Hall of India.
4. Booch G. (1994), Object Oriented Analysis & Design with Application, 2nd Edition, Addison-Wesley Publication.
5. Brooks, P. F., Jr. (2006), *The Mythical Man-Month*, Pearson Education.
6. Budgen, David (1994), *Software Design*, Addison Wesley.
7. Dennis A. and Wixom, B.H. (2002), *System Analysis & Design*, John Wiley & Sons, Inc.
8. Fowler Martin , *What's a Model for?*
9. Fowler Martin , *Who needs an Architect?*
10. Gill, Nasib Singh (2002), *Software Engineering-Software Reliability, Testing and Quality Assurance*, Khanna Book Publishing Co. (P) Ltd.
11. Hall, A. (1990), *Seven Myths of Formal Methods*, IEEE Software, 7(5), 11-20.
12. Hwang K. (2001), *Advanced Computer Architecture-Parallelism, Scalability, Programmability*, Tata McGraw Hill.

13. J.J. Marchiniak, "*Encyclopedia of Software Engineering*", John-Wiley & Sons (Vol. I), 1994

14. Jacobson I. (1999), *Object Oriented Software Engineering*, Addison-Wesley.

15. Jain Deepak (2004), *OOPS compatibility in VHDL.*

16. Jain Deepak (2004), *D-FOM: Yet Another Object Model*

17. Jain Deepak (2005), *UML: What, Why & How*, DIAS Times, July-September 2005 issue pp 29-31.

18. Jain Deepak (2006), *UML: What, Why & How*, DIAS Times.

19. Jalote, P. (2005), *An Integrated Approach to Software Engineering*, 3rd Edition, Narosa Publishing House, New Delhi.

20. Mall Rajib (1999), *Fundamentals of Software Engineering*, Prentice Hall of India, New Delhi.

21. Michael A. Ogush, Derek Coleman, Dorothea Beringer (2000), *A Template for Documenting Software and Firmware Architectures,* (Version 1.3, 15-Mar-00)

22. Navabi Z. (1998), *VHDL: Analysis and Modeling of Digital System*, 2nd Edition, McGraw Hill Company, New York

23. Pfleeger S.L. (1998), *Software Engineering*, Prentice-Hall International, Inc.

24. Pressman Roger S. (1997), *Software Engineering: A Practitioner's Approach*, 4th Edition, Tata McGraw Hill.

25. Quatrani Terry (2000), *Visual Modeling with Rational Rose 2000 and UML,* Addison Wesley.

26. Richard C. Lee, William M. Tepfenhart (2005), *UML and C++*, A Practical Guide to Object Oriented Development, 2nd Edition, Prentice-Hall of India.

27. Rumbaugh, J., Blaha M., Premerlani W. and Eddy F., (1998), *Object Oriented Analysis & Design*, Prentice Hall of India.

28. S.H. Kan (1995), *Metrics and Models in Software Quality Engineering*, Addison-Wesley.

29. SEI (1996), *Managing Software Development with Metrics*, Course material.

30. Shepperd M. (1995), *Foundations of Software Measurement*, Prentice Hall.